EAST LONDON SUFFRAGETTES

SARAH JACKSON AND ROSEMARY TAYLOR

The History Press

D1206431

First published 2014

The History Press
The Mill, Brimscombe Port
Stroud, Gloucestershire, GL5 2QG
www.thehistorypress.co.uk

British Library Cataloguing in Publication Data.
A catalogue record for this book is available from the British Library.

ISBN 978 0 7509 6093 9

Typesetting and origination by The History Press
Printed in Great Britain

CONTENTS

INTRODUCTION

In July 2012 the suffragettes were finally awarded their proper place on the stage of British history. In the midst of a national celebration watched by millions, a group of women in Edwardian dress, wearing sashes and bearing 'Votes for Women' banners, stepped on to the AstroTurf of the Olympic stadium in Stratford.

But how many of those in the Olympic boroughs know the role played by the suffragettes on their doorstep, 100 years ago? This book aims to tell the story of the East London Federation of the Suffragettes and some of the remarkable women behind their fascinating projects and campaigns, including their leader, Sylvia Pankhurst.

One

THE EAST END

Of course London has had an east as long as it has had a centre, but the 'East End' didn't form in the popular imagination until the late nineteenth century, when industrialisation and the social changes which followed in its wake caused the area's remaining middle-class families to flee to the suburbs. After more than a century of fame (and infamy), Bow, Stepney, Whitechapel, Bethnal Green, Poplar and Wapping feel familiar even to those who have never set foot in them.

To many respectable middle- and upper-class Londoners in the late 1800s and early 1900s, the East End seemed to be at once on their doorstep, and a kind of foreign country. With its poverty, disease, slums and sweated industries, it was too close for comfort, and many feared that the political activism, industrial action and religious dissent which were also a hallmark of the area would seep westward. In 1891, writer John Henry Mackay described the East End as 'a hell of poverty. Like an enormous, black, motionless kraken, the poverty of London lies there in silence and encircles with its mighty tentacles the life and wealth of the city and of the West End.'

At the same time, the harsh living and working conditions experienced by many of the East End's community seemed unimaginable and nightmarish. The inhabitants themselves were subject to intense prejudice. One journal from 1888 observed that 'A shabby man from Paddington, Marylebone or Battersea might pass muster as one of the respectable poor. But the same man coming from Bethnal Green, Shadwell or Wapping was an "East Ender"; the box of … bug powder must be reached for, and the spoons locked up.'

Despite these fears, the East End fascinated many in London and beyond. It represented more than a geographic area, becoming a symbolic battleground for a host of conflicting ideas about work, home, health, identity, democracy and religion.

Poverty

The thick black lines on Charles Booth's map of London memorably visualise the poverty which was one of the defining characteristics of East London at the end of the nineteenth century. Victorian philanthropists and reformers, including William Booth and Octavia Hill, had campaigned to raise awareness, alleviate suffering, and improve conditions. Despite this, the East End into which Sylvia Pankhurst arrived in 1906 was not greatly changed from the days of Charles Dickens. In 1895 German anarchist Rudolf Rocker visited Tower Hamlets to observe and document the conditions in which people lived and worked, which he described in *The London Years*:

There were at that time thousands of people in London who had never slept in a bed, who just crept into some filthy hole where the police would not disturb them. I saw with my own eyes thousands of human beings who can hardly still be considered such, people who were no longer capable of any kind of work. They went about in foul rags, through which their skin showed, dirty and lousy, never free from hunger, starving, scavenging their food out of dustbins and the refuse heaps that were left behind after the markets closed.

There were squalid courts and alley-ways, with dreary tumble-down hovels, whose stark despair it is impossible to describe. And in these cesspools of poverty children were born and people lived, struggling all their lives with poverty and pain, shunned like lepers by all 'decent' members of society.

While Rocker's account is typical of many examples of 'slum literature' in that it dehumanises the East End's inhabitants – they are described as a mass of animal-like creatures, without individual faces, names or voices – it paints a vivid picture of the squalor in which people were forced to live.

In the notorious overcrowded slums, families were housed in single rooms, with only a single outside lavatory and a water pump shared with several houses. Many of the buildings were falling into disrepair, with broken stairs, peeling wallpaper, or chunks of plaster pulling away from the ceiling. The slums were also full of vermin – black beetles, bed bugs and rats were perpetual unwanted guests of the human tenants.

Disease was an inevitable consequence of such living conditions. There were repeated outbreaks of cholera in East London during the nineteenth century, including a very severe epidemic in 1866 in which more than 5,000 people died. Infant mortality was also extremely high, reaching 250 infant deaths per 1,000 live births in some of the worst slums, such as the notorious Old Nichol in Shoreditch.

At this time doctors charged a fee and medicine was expensive. In 1911, as part of a wave of reforms, the Liberal government introduced National Health Insurance (a forerunner of the National Health Service) for employees earning less than £160 per year. The worker contributed 4d, the employer contributed 3d and the government 2d, which provided sickness benefit entitlement of 9s, free medical treatment and maternity benefit of 30s. Although an estimated 13 million workers came to be covered under this scheme the new provisions still only benefited a small portion of the population. For example, a man might be covered through his workplace, but his family would not be.

Another crucial factor which contributed to poor health was a lack of adequate food for nutrition, or even for survival. Starvation was a real and insistent danger facing the poorest inhabitants of East London, as this excerpt from Jack London's 1903 book *The People of the Abyss* reveals:

The Carter was hard put to keep the pace at which we walked (he told me that he had eaten nothing that day), but the Carpenter, lean and hungry, his grey and ragged overcoat flapping mournfully in the breeze, swung on in a long and tireless stride which reminded me strongly of the plains wolf or coyote. Both kept their eyes upon the pavement as they walked and talked, and every now and then one or the other would stoop and pick something up, never missing the stride the while. I thought it was cigar and cigarette stumps they were collecting, and for some time took no notice. Then I did notice.

From the slimy, spittle-drenched sidewalk, they were picking up bits of orange peel, apple skin, and grape stems, and they were eating them. The pits of greengage plums they cracked between their teeth for the kernels inside. They picked up stray bits of bread the size of peas, apple cores so black and dirty one would not take them to be apple cores, and these things these two men took into their mouths, and chewed them, and swallowed them; and this, between six and seven o'clock in the evening of August 20, year of our Lord 1902, in the heart of the greatest, wealthiest, and most powerful empire the world has ever seen.

As one of its raft of reforms, the Liberal government had introduced free school meals for the poorest pupils in 1906, but had crucially failed to enforce the measure, instead allowing Local Education Authorities to decide whether or not to take up the scheme. By 1912 only half of all councils in the country had done so.

Poverty forced many children out of school at an early age, especially girls, for whom education was not viewed as a necessity. One 1899 report looked at regular part-time work done by boys and girls. Girls, all aged 6, were employed in the following ways:

Occupation	Hours per week	Wages per week
Errands	9	6d
Minding Neighbour's Baby	Every evening 7 to 8 pm	1d
" " "	Every Saturday	1d
Cleaning	Saturday – few hours	2d
Minding baby	7 hours	Tea and ½d
Window cleaning	4 hours	1d plus dinner and tea
Lace work	6 to 8 hours	Helps mother
Matchbox making	6 hours	2½d per gross
Carrying meals	5 hours	3d
Taking out groceries	15 hours	2d

Older children worked long hours before and after school, delivering milk, selling newspapers, working in shops and doing domestic work, earning an average of 1 ½d an hour. At this time a loaf of bread cost around 12d (twelve pence, or one shilling).

At the turn of the century, secondary education was still not available to working-class children. However, in 1907 free places were offered to very able pupils for further studies. Even then the Board of Education recommended that girls over 15 years of age should study Practical Housewifery: 'We do not think it desirable to attempt to divorce a girl's education from her home duties and home opportunities.' What exactly was meant by 'home opportunities' is not clear. By 1910 the Board of Education had outlined in greater detail the curriculum to be followed by 12 and 13-year-old girls in elementary school: personal hygiene, temperance, home nursing, housekeeping and infant care.

Industry

The social, economic and cultural character of the East End was enormously influenced by the major industries located there, industries which both women and men worked in their thousands. Many worked on and around the Thames docks, on the ships, loading and unloading cargo at East and West India Quays and Wapping, as ropemakers, as packers, and in great factories producing items which were shipped all over the world.

Margaret Harkness, who published her work under the name of John Law, carried out extensive research on women's labour in the East End. She wrote:

So far I have found that there are at least 200 trades at which girls work in the city, namely, brush-makers, button-makers, cigarette-makers, electric light fitters, fur workers, India rubber stamp machinists, magic lantern slide makers, perfumers, portmanteau makers, spectacle makers, surgical instrument makers, tie makers etc.

These girls can be roughly divided into two classes: those who earn from 8s to 14s, and those who earn from 4s to 8s a week. Taking slack time into consideration, it is, I think, safe to say that 10s is the average weekly wage for the first class and 4s 6d that of the second class. Their weekly wages often fall below this, and sometime rise above it.

The hours are almost invariably from 8 am to 7 pm with one hour for dinner and a half holiday on Saturday. I know few cases in which such girls work less; a good many in which overtime reaches to 10 or 11 at night; a few in which overtime means all night. There is little to choose between the two classes. The second are allowed by their employers to wear old clothes and boots, the first must make a 'genteel appearance' ... how the girls have to stint on underclothing and food in order to make what their employers call a 'genteel appearance!' Many a family is at the present kept by the labour of one or two such girls, who can at the most earn a few shillings.

The East End has a long association with the textile industry, which can be traced back to the wave of Huguenot silkmakers who settled in and around Spitalfields in the late 1600s. At the end of the 1800s, the clothing industry in East London was notorious for using 'sweated' labour, exploiting large numbers of mostly Jewish and Irish immigrant workers who had little choice but to work for a pittance in terrible conditions. An extract from *The Lancet* in 1884 reads:

> In Hanbury Street we found 18 workers crowded in a small room measuring 8 yards by 4½ yards and not quite 8½ feet high … The top room had at times to hold 18 persons, working in the heat and gas of the stove, warming the pressing irons, surrounded by mounds of dust and remnants of the cut cloth, breathing an atmosphere full of woollen particles containing more or less injurious dyes. It is not surprising that so large a proportion of working tailors break down from diseases of the respiratory system.

At this time in the East End many businesses also heavily exploited huge numbers of homeworkers, most of whom were women. Making matchboxes, taking in laundry or sewing work were common tasks, and the women were forced to work punishing hours to make ends meet. One of the most famous cultural representations of this form of sweated labour was a poem by Thomas Hood, called 'The Song of the Shirt', which appeared in *Punch* magazine in 1843. Here is an excerpt:

> Work--work--work
> Till the brain begins to swim;
> Work--work--work
> Till the eyes are heavy and dim!
> Seam, and gusset, and band,
> Band, and gusset, and seam,
> Till over the buttons I fall asleep,
> And sew them on in a dream!

Oh, Men, with Sisters dear!

Oh, Men, with Mothers and Wives!

It is not linen you're wearing out,

But human creatures' lives!

Stitch--stitch--stitch,

In poverty, hunger and dirt,

Sewing at once, with a double thread,

A Shroud as well as a Shirt.

Immigration

No other area of Britain has experienced the same degree of changing population as the East End of London, as successive waves of immigrants and refugees sought shelter or opportunity in the shadow of the Tower of London: French Huguenots, Germans, Irish, Jews, Chinese, West Indians, Indians and Bangladeshis. Each group in turn has introduced its own individual mode of working and living, building their own places of worship and houses, adapting their environment to suit their needs. Having established themselves, the newly affluent tended to migrate to the suburbs in the north and east of London, their dwellings and shops being taken over by the next generation of refugees.

The diversity of East London in the second half of the nineteenth century, and also the breathtaking racism of most Victorians, is evident in this description of 'Tiger Bay' (modern-day Shadwell) from *The Pauper, The Thief and the Convict* (1865) by Thomas Archer, who was horrified to see:

> ... colonies of Irish, hordes of Germans, burrowing in the wretched tenements and swarming from roof to basement, the children wallowing in dirt, and clothed in tatters ... A cellar

where four lascars roll their yellow and black eyes upon us as they glare silently at each other, and smoke from one bamboo pipe ... Rooms, where dark-skinned, snakelike Hindoos (beggars and tract-sellers by day) live with English and Irish women as their wives ... yellow Chinese sit in the midst of filth upon a heap of rags or on a dislocated couch, the refuse of a neighbouring broker's shop, and stupefy themselves with opium, while their two or three wives quarrel or fight, or cook a modicum of rice and pork over the embers of a wretched fire ...

In Archer's deliberately titillating account we can see the seeds of many of the damaging myths and racist stereotypes which surround immigration in our own day. As Sukdhev Sandhu points out in his book *London Calling: How Black and Asian Writers Imagined a City*:

The East End in which blacks lived became synonymous in Victorian times with spiritual degradation. It was a man-trap, a Satanic stronghold, a dumping ground for human flotsam. It wasn't just that the area was blighted by poverty; the colour of its inhabitants encouraged reactionaries to see it as a place of contamination, of moral canker. The problem was one of poor (racial) hygiene. In sensationalist newspaper reports as well as in the accounts of social workers, it was seen as a dark zone which needed Christian reclamation just as urgently as those heathen lands thousands of miles away which were being penetrated by explorers and missionaries ...

While the racism of many contemporary accounts leaves a sour taste in the mouth, it is important to emphasise that the East End has been an ethnically diverse area for many hundreds of years, despite the whitewashing at work in much local history. For example, the practice of employing South Asian 'lascars' to work British ships (and then refusing to pay for their return passage) meant that from the 1700s onwards there was an Asian community in East London. Although most of the Asian people living in London at this time were men, there are numerous examples in parish records of marriages with local women, and mixed race families were not uncommon.

Between 1880 and 1914, many Jewish migrants from Poland, Germany and Russia came into the East End, many fleeing the pogroms in those countries, others looking to improve their working prospects. There were also large numbers of people arriving from Ireland, escaping cruel English landlords and waves of famine. Many African and Caribbean workers also travelled to Britain at this time, and settled in the East End. One of the most famous is Donald Adolphus Brown, who married East London suffragette Adelaide Knight and in 1921 was awarded a medal for bravery, as the *London Gazette* records:

> His Majesty the King has been graciously pleased to award the Edward Medal to Mr. Donald Adolphus Brown, Foreman, R.N.O. Depot, Woolwich, under the following circumstances :—

> On January 7th, 1919, while a number of rockets and lights were being re-packed at the Royal Naval Ordnance Depot at Woolwich, one of the rockets ignited and exploded, thus causing other rockets in the same case to explode. Brown, a foreman in the Ordnance Depot, immediately threw water upon the flaming case, opened the doors of the storehouse and dragged the case into the open. This he did single-handed, but as a result of his example, other employees came to his assistance, and the fire was eventually extinguished by the use of fire buckets and a portable pump.

The storehouse was full of fireworks and flares of every description, and there was a large store of detonators immediately adjoining; several hundred men and women were at work in the immediate vicinity, and had it not been for the promptitude and determination shown by Brown, there is no doubt that a very serious explosion would have occurred. Brown was fully aware of the fact that the store was full of explosives, and of the danger which he was running, and by his courageous act he certainly saved many lives.

Radicals

At the turn of the century East London (from Clerkenwell out) was well established as a hub of radical political philosophy and activism. Public halls and parks attracted socialist and anarchist speakers from around the world, including Rosa Luxembourg, Emma Goldman, Peter Kropotkin and Lenin. British socialist feminists Beatrice Webb and Annie Besant were also active in the area, speaking, campaigning and conducting research.

Eleanor Marx, daughter of Karl Marx, was a regular visitor to East London where she addressed large public meetings of several thousand people. Eleanor spoke out on a wide range of issues, including campaigning against anti-Semitism. She was open about her own Jewish heritage and learnt Yiddish so that she could help the Jewish working women of Whitechapel to organise.

Most of all Eleanor was involved in building up the fledgling trade-union movement. She also played an important role in the formation of the Gas Workers and General Labourers' Union, helping leader Will Thorne to draw up the new union's constitution and taking special responsibility for two of its branches which represented women workers. Marx worked closely with Thorne to lead the union to a decisive victory. They secured an eight-hour day for workers at the Gas, Light & Coke Co. in East Ham in 1889, a milestone in trade union history. In the same year she helped to organise the Dockers' Strike, in which 100,000 dock workers went on strike over pay cuts, and won.

Another campaigner spreading radical ideas in the East End at the end of the nineteenth century was Keir Hardie, who would become a key supporter of the East London Federation of the Suffragettes. In 1892 West Ham had entered the history books when Keir Hardie was elected as the first Independent Labour Party MP. He shocked the country by taking his place in the House of Commons wearing a cloth cap and tweed suit, rather than the traditional black coat and silk top hat. As an MP he argued that people earning more than a £1,000 a year should pay more tax, and that the extra revenue should be used to provide old-age pensions and free schooling for the workers. Hardie also campaigned for Parliamentary reform, including the abolition of the House of Lords.

Hardie was born in Lanarkshire, the illegitimate son of a servant who later married a ship's carpenter and moved to Glasgow with her son. From the age of 8 he worked as a baker's delivery boy and then, from age 11, as a miner. He never attended school, and only learnt to read in his teens. Hardie helped to establish a union at the colliery where he worked, and was dismissed for leading a strike. He began work at the Scottish Miners' Federation and published a newspaper, called *The Miner*, which later became *Labour Leader*.

In 1888 Hardie met and became friends with the Pankhursts, who persuaded him of the importance of women's suffrage. Later, when Sylvia Pankhurst was in her mid-twenties and studying at the Royal College of Art in London she began a relationship with Hardie, despite the thirty year age difference between them and the fact that Hardie was already married. Their deep friendship lasted until Hardie died in 1915, and he acted as a mentor and an important supporter of Sylvia's work and the wider movement.

Reinforced by his personal ties to the movement, Hardie's support for women's suffrage stemmed from deeply held principles of justice and equality. In 1907 Keir Hardie told the Labour Party conference:

> I thought the days of my pioneering were over but of late I have felt, with increasing intensity, the injustice inflicted on women by our present laws. The [Labour] Party is largely my own child and I cannot part from it lightly, or without pain; but at the same time I cannot sever myself from the principles I hold. If it is necessary for me to separate myself from what has been my life's work, I do so in order to remove the stigma resting upon our wives, mothers and sisters of being accounted unfit for citizenship.

Marx and Hardie are just two names on a long list of individuals who spread socialist, feminist or anarchist ideas from a wooden platform in the East End's beloved Vicky Park. As soon as it opened in 1845 Victoria Park became the scene of huge meetings, mass rallies and speeches by a long list of luminaries, including: Annie Besant, George Lansbury, William Morris, George Bernard Shaw, Millicent Fawcett and countless others. An attempt was made to ban public meetings in the park without written permission in 1862, but was entirely ignored, as was a later attempt in 1888 to prohibit collections during the open-air meetings.

This 1872 ode captures some of the pride and affection in which the park was held by local workers (author unknown):

The East End

The Park is called the People's Park
And all the walks are theirs
And strolling through the flowery paths
They breathe exotic airs,
South Kensington, let it remain
Among the Upper Ten.
East London, with useful things,
Be left with working men.

The rich should ponder on the fact
Tis labour has built it up
A mountain of prodigious wealth
And filled the golden cup.
And surely workers who have toiled
Are worthy to behold
Some portion of the treasures won
And ribs of shining gold.

Two

WOMEN'S ACTIVISM IN THE EAST END

The story of women's activism in East London doesn't begin with the suffragettes. Women participated in and led different kinds of campaigns in the decades before the suffragettes arrived, from the early suffrage movement to local politics and civic life to industrial action. Women, like men, were speaking out for a better, fairer future.

Suffrage societies

I may excite laughter by dropping a hint, which I mean to pursue some future time, for I really think that women ought to have representatives, instead of being arbitrarily governed, without having any direct share allowed them in the deliberations of Government.

But, as the whole system of representation is now in this country only a convenient handle for despotism, they need not complain, for they are as well represented as a numerous class of hard-working mechanics, who pay for the support of royalty when they can scarcely stop their children's mouths with bread.

Mary Wollstonecraft, in her *A Vindication of the Rights of Women*, 1792.

At the start of the nineteenth century very few people in Britain had the right to vote. One survey in 1780 showed just 214,000 people made up the Electorate of England and Wales, less than 3 per cent of the total population. In the 1790s, influenced by works such as Thomas Paine's *Rights of Man,* reformers began to demand that all men be given the right to vote.

Bowing to increasing pressure and fear of revolution, three parliamentary reform Acts were passed, in 1832, 1867 and 1884, which gradually extended the vote. It was slow progress. The 1832 Act gave the vote only to men who held property with an annual value of £10, which excluded the vast majority. After the second reform act, only two in every five men had the vote. Even the third Reform Act in 1884, which delivered the vote to all men who owned a house, and added 6 million people to the voting register, still excluded huge numbers of men, and of course, all women.

From the 1860s onwards local groups and clubs calling for women's suffrage sprang up around the country, including many in the predominantly working-class Lancashire mill towns. Several of these societies combined to form the National Union of Women's Suffrage Societies in 1897, led by the formidable Millicent Fawcett.

When Millicent was a teenager, her older sister, Elizabeth Garrett, moved to London to study medicine, going on to be Britain's first qualified woman doctor. Millicent's visits to London to stay with Elizabeth brought her into contact with people with radical political views, including John Stuart Mill and her future husband Henry Fawcett, Liberal MP for Brighton.

As well as using her superb organisational skills to advance the cause of women's suffrage, Millicent wrote popular books on politics, helped to found Newnham College at Cambridge University, and led a government commission to investigate the appalling conditions in which prisoners of war were being kept in South Africa during the Boer War.

Although she never participated in the militant actions of the suffragettes, she admired their courage. In 1906 she helped to organise a banquet at the Savoy Hotel to celebrate the release of Women's Social and Political Union (WSPU) prisoners from Holloway Prison. Fawcett and the NUWSS are often cast as the sensible older sisters to the militant suffragettes, laying the vital foundations for victory. By the standards of the time the constitutional suffragists were also bold, outspoken and courageous. And they were determined. Fawcett herself said in a speech in 1911 that their movement was 'like a glacier; slow moving but unstoppable'.

East London had its share of activism for women's suffrage. For example, a Women's Suffrage Society meeting at Stratford Town Hall is reported in the *Stratford Express* in 1887. And by 1905 it is clear that there was a great deal of activity in the area, led by working women. One of the most important figures was Minnie Baldock, the wife of a fitter who lived in Canning Town. As a girl she had worked in a factory, and in the first years of the 1900s she was a local guardian and a suffrage activist. A letter to her friend and comrade Dora Montefiore in 1905 provides a good example of the activities that local women were undertaking in the name of votes for women:

We went to a crowded meeting held at the Poplar Town Hall, we sat in about the middle of the hall and listened very attentively to the Chairman and S.B. [Sydney Buxton, the local Liberal candidate], but no reference was made to women. So my friend stood up and asked S.B. if he was returned would he give votes to women, but received no answer. She then stood on her seat and held up a flag she had made. White with red letters 'Votes for Women.' She made me laugh, for she turned round like a spinning top so that everybody could see, and would not get down until the stewards came to her and asked her to go on the platform; they could not turn her out as the place was so packed.

I was rather sorry at the time that she consented, but they gave her a chair on the front and told her they would answer her question. They then asked for questions; my friend then placed her banner over her knees so that for the rest of the evening everyone could see it. When S.B. answered he said he could not vote for Woman Suffrage, they could not sit in Parliament, and he did not believe in them having a vote for where they could not sit. (As if they could not amend the law.) They talked to us and about us as if we were fools indeed. I was ready to answer him that way, but my friend had sent me a note saying that S.B. would allow me to say a few words about W.S., if I was connected with the constituency, as if it was not a national question.

I was so glad, for I just felt fit and I held that united manifesto in favour of votes for women in my hands. I was going to mention what Mazzini said about women and tell them that we wanted power to help ourselves, etc. I should have read the manifesto to them, but I waited in vain. They closed the meeting without calling upon me. I shall know better next time than to believe their logic. We made an impression, anyhow, and my friend was cheered for her bravery by some men.

She goes on to invite Dora to speak at a number of upcoming meetings. Minnie's letter hints at a bold and well-informed activist base in East London, long before the suffragettes.

Matchmakers and trade unions

Another arena for women's activism was the trade-union movement and other forms of collective action to improve working conditions. The Matchwomen's Strike in 1888 was the most famous strike by women workers, and launched a great wave of industrial unrest. World-famous at the time, it has long been relegated to the footnotes of labour history. Happily its true significance is now being recovered.

Matchmaking was a major industry in the East End of London. Thousands of girls and women worked long hours, standing at benches making matches and matchboxes. Women worked 14 hours a day for less than 5s a week, and didn't often receive this, thanks to a system of fines for offences including talking, dropping matches or going to the toilet without permission. Thousands more worked with their young children at home, labouring long into the night to produce their quota of boxes.

In the factories the women and girls worked with the dangerous yellow phosphorus, which was used for the match heads. Phosphorus covered the benches they worked at, and during their dinner hour they ate their lunches at the same benches. Phosphorus also covered their clothes so that they were luminous in the dark. A number of girls had yellow, jaundiced skin through inhaling the phosphorus fumes. Inhaling the fumes also caused coughing, shortness of breath, chest pains, and congestion of the lungs, nausea, vomiting and ultimately liver failure. In the dark winter evenings, the gutters around Bow glowed with luminous vomit, evidence that the girls had finished work for the week.

Many of the women workers suffered with a condition known as 'phossy jaw'. The technical term was 'necrosis', meaning the decay of bone tissue in the jaw, causing disfigurement, terrible pain and suffering. In some cases the condition was fatal, but there are scant records available of the numbers who suffered and died from this dreadful affliction.

In June of 1888, the Fabian Society met to discuss the conditions of the workers at the Bryant and May factory in Bow. Clementina Black had presented a paper on the working conditions of the girls at the factory, and compared their situation to that of the shareholders of the company, who that year had been awarded dividends of 38 per cent. Annie Besant agreed to investigate the plight of the matchwomen and on 23 June she published an article in *The Link* entitled 'White Slavery in London'. In it she exposed the working conditions at the Bryant and May factory, based on interviews with some of the girls. Frederick Bryant responded by claiming that Annie Besant was spreading lies. To this she retorted, 'Then sue me for libel.'

The management of the factory hunted for the women who had spoken to Besant, and they were asked to sign a paper stating that the account was a lie. The women refused to do so, and one – held to be their leader – was dismissed. A deputation of women to the management demanded her reinstatement, which was refused, and so about 1,200 women and men walked out.

The news made the national papers and questions were asked in Parliament. Public opinion was solidly behind the strikers. Meetings were held at Mile End Waste and in Hyde Park, and offers of financial support poured in. Among the embarrassing revelations of the working practices employed at the factory, and profits enjoyed by the shareholders, the management caved in and the dispute was settled.

Countless women-led strikes were to follow over the next twenty years. In 1911, 15,000 women in Bermondsey,

South East London came out on strike against low wages and bad working conditions in the district. The strike, which affected thirty firms, secured many concessions including a rise in wages at Pinks' jam factory from 9 to 11s a week. In 1914, 300 women workers of Messrs C. and E. Morton, Millwall, came out on strike to protest against the employment of four young girls of between 14 and 15 years of age being put on to press work in the tin-box making section of the factory at a low wage. The strike lasted twelve days before the management caved in and agreed to the strikers' demands.

Despite these examples of women fighting back against exploitation (and winning!), the trade-union movement at the end of the nineteenth century was generally sceptical or even hostile towards women's employment rights and their right to vote. Women workers were perceived as a threat to men's employment, as it was thought bosses would hire women on cheaper rates to do men's work. Then as now, many otherwise radical activists adhered to the traditional idea of 'separate spheres', in which women's domain was the home and men's the workplace. Given these attitudes, it is not surprising that even after the huge increase in union membership among women in the first decade of the twentieth century, by 1914 90 per cent of all trade unionists were men and less than 10 per cent of women were unionised. In an attempt to address the lack of unionisation among women workers, and combat the sexism evident in the labour movement, Mary MacArthur created the National Federation of Women Workers (NFWW), bringing together several women's unions. By 1914 its membership had risen to 20,000. The NFWW also campaigned effectively against sweated labour, managing to persuade the Liberal government to pass the 1909 Trade Boards Act which attempted to fix minimum wages in some of the most exploitative industries, which tended to be the ones which mostly employed women.

Local politics and civic life

Women were also active in local political and civic life, as local councillors, Poor Law guardians, members of school boards and as charity trustees.

Women won the right to vote in local council elections in 1894, and were permitted to stand as local councillors following the Qualification of Women Act in 1907. The newly formed Independent Labour Party presented more opportunities for women to participate in local politics than the more traditional Liberal or Conservative parties, and many women who played a key role in the East London Federation of the Suffragettes were Labour councillors, guardians or committee members.

Henrietta 'Nettie' Adler was one of the first women to be elected as a local councillor, for the Central Hackney Division of the London County Council in 1910. Nettie was the daughter of the Chief Rabbi and an activist in the Jewish community around Hackney. According to the election leaflet, she had been 'interested for many years in social questions affecting the welfare of women and children and especially in matters relating to the industrial status of women workers'. Before standing, she had been a school manager for twenty years. She represented Central Hackney on the London County Council for over fifteen years. In 1920 she was appointed Justice of the Peace and in 1921 was selected by the Lord Chancellor to serve on the rota of the Shoreditch Juvenile Court.

Many women also played an important formal role in their communities as Poor Law guardians. In 1834 the Poor Law

Amendment Act was passed, which included a provision for taxpayers in each parish to elect a Board of Guardians who would be responsible for supervising the feared and hated workhouse, collecting the Poor Rate and sending reports to the Central Poor Law Commission. Women were permitted to stand as guardians in 1894, which allowed many to effect change in their communities, and to provide direct assistance to some of the most vulnerable people in society.

Julia Scurr was born in Limehouse, the daughter of an Irish immigrant, and married John Scurr, an Australian immigrant, in 1900. Sharing the same radical politics and a determination to improve the lives of working people in the East End, they made a formidable partnership. In 1907 Julia was elected to the Poplar Board of Guardians, and would remain a guardian until she died. In June 1912 she presented a report criticising the lack of day rooms and recreational space at the Bow Infirmary (later St Clement's Hospital), stating that the residents had no choice but to stand around in unheated corridors. One man was refused discharge because he had no clothes. Julia reminded the governors that it was an infirmary, not a place of detention. Her male colleagues dismissed the report as being exaggerated. Julia became well known and respected throughout East London after organising food for the children of strikers during the 1912 dock strike. She also worked to improve the rights of the Irish community and became heavily involved with the women's suffrage movement and the East London Federation of the Suffragettes.

In the year before the WSPU arrived in Canning Town, Julia Scurr organised a mass demonstration by women. In July 1905, with socialist activists Keir Hardie, George Lansbury and Dora Montefiore, Julia organised a march of 1,000 women from the East End to Westminster to lobby for welfare provision for the unemployed. Later that year, in November, another march took place: 4,000 women married to unemployed men from Poplar, Southwark and West Ham marched down Whitehall, accompanied by a band playing 'The Marseillaise' and bearing banners that read 'Food for Our Children', 'Work for Our Men', and 'Workers of the World Unite'.

Second-class citizens

Reading these stories it is easy to forget that the dominant view of the time was that women were intellectually inferior to men, and too weak to handle even a small amount of power. Most women of the day were prevented from fulfilling their potential by these deeply entrenched ideas.

At the start of the twentieth century, despite a modest wave of legal changes in the previous two decades, women were still second-class citizens. Women could not inherit, hold or dispose of property on equal terms to men; they were barred from the legal and accounting professions; they could not sit on juries; they did not have equal rights to be guardians of their children; they could not obtain a divorce as easily as men; while trapped in a sexual double standard they could not easily access contraception or information about family planning; they were paid half a man's wages for the same work. And of course, they couldn't vote.

Three

EARLY SUFFRAGETTE ACTIVITY IN EAST LONDON

The suffragette movement, distinct from the wider suffrage movement, began in Manchester with the formation of the Women's Social and Political Union (WSPU) in October 1903, led by Mrs Emmeline Pankhurst and her oldest daughter Christabel. Younger daughters Adela and Sylvia were actively involved in the WSPU at the start but eventually chose different paths.

The Women's Social and Political Union

The small group of women who founded the WSPU had been previously involved in suffrage campaigns and societies, the largest of which was the National Union of Women's Suffrage Societies, but became increasingly frustrated at the lack of progress which had been made by trying to engage with politicians through meetings and petitions. The WSPU's founding members decided that they would found a women-only campaigning organisation which would work with the Independent Labour Party to secure social and parliamentary reforms which they found continually denied to them by the Liberal Party and the Conservative government. As a last straw they had recently discovered that women would not be permitted to hold or attend meetings in the new Pankhurst Hall, which had been built in honour of Mrs Pankhurst's late husband, Dr Richard Pankhurst, and which Sylvia had worked hard to decorate.

Many of the early supporters of the WSPU were working-class women, and the new movement built on the work of Esther Roper, Eva Gore Booth and others in gaining support for women's suffrage among women trade unionists in the North of England. After yet another bill calling for women's suffrage was thrown out of Parliament in 1905, the WSPU began to focus entirely on securing the vote. They abandoned their plans to campaign for social reforms, pledged to target whichever political party was in government and refused to support any legislation which did not award women the vote.

Although the WSPU used a huge range of different campaign tactics and tools, they are most remembered for the courageous individual acts of militancy which shocked the nation into paying attention to 'the woman question'. From chaining themselves to railings, committing arson, throwing flour bombs, enduring hunger strikes, to Emily Wilding Davison's sacrifice when she threw herself under the King's horse at the 1913 Epsom Derby, these acts have gone down in history. However, the WSPU were not militant from the beginning, and their actions gradually became more extreme. In the early years of militancy, the actions of the WSPU were closer to traditional forms of protest and civil disobedience than violence and terrorism.

Sylvia Pankhurst

Estelle Sylvia Pankhurst was born in Manchester on 5 May 1882 to Richard and Emmeline Pankhurst. Although the Pankhursts were a middle-class family, they held left-wing political views and had many progressive ideas, including support for women's suffrage. They were involved in numerous campaigns and social reform projects, and in 1889 they were part of the group of radicals who formed the Women's Franchise League.

When Richard Pankhurst died in 1897, Sylvia was very deeply affected. She dedicated her life to furthering their shared socialist ideals, and often returned to memories of her father's beliefs and actions as a guide in her adult life. Although Sylvia and her mother later grew apart, it is clear that Emmeline also had a tremendous influence on her – not least in providing a model of courage and determination, and the ability to inspire and organise for which the Pankhursts are rightly famous. Speaking in a BBC interview in 1953, Sylvia recalled that 'to all of us at home in my childhood, she was the most marvellous and beautiful woman in the world'.

Supported by their parents to pursue their interests and develop their natural talents, Christabel trained as a lawyer, Sylvia won a scholarship at the Royal College of Art, and Adela became a teacher. While Christabel and Sylvia both played very high-profile roles in the suffrage movement, Adela's contribution is less well recognised. She was an enthusiastic and committed WSPU organiser, and although she later emigrated to Australia she continued to campaign there for women's rights, as well as join the peace movement.

For Sylvia, like her sisters, the struggle for women's rights gradually took precedence and she channelled her gift into designing posters, banners, and badges. Sylvia's talent as an artist and designer is clearly visible in the beauty and quality of the WSPU materials, and her socialist ideals are discernible in some of the early items. For example, the WSPU membership card features a group of women who are clearly workers and not upper-class ladies. Artefacts like this, combined with the origins of the WSPU in the labour movement and early support from the working-class women of East London, just show how far the WSPU leaders moved from left to right between 1903 and 1914.

However, Sylvia Pankhurst followed an entirely different trajectory which eventually caused a deep rift with her mother and sister Christabel. After moving to Bow in 1912 to lead the WSPU's East End campaign, she was deeply moved by the plight of the poverty-stricken women she met there, and came to see the struggle for women to have the vote as just one strand in a larger struggle for equality. She recognised that the day-to-day concerns of local women were part of this struggle. How could women campaign for the vote when they needed to work to feed their children? Why should they work exclusively towards votes for women when their husbands also did not have the vote? Sylvia and the East London branch of the WSPU began to look for practical answers to these questions and connect women's suffrage to other issues, a move which the WSPU leadership refused to tolerate. It is a testament to Sylvia's commitment that when asked to choose between her family and her 'mates' in the East End, she chose the latter.

For the next ten years, Sylvia lived and worked in East London, driving numerous projects and campaigns to win universal suffrage and equal pay, to relieve poverty and suffering, to support working mothers, to combat fascism and racism, and to protect workers' rights. While Sylvia Pankhurst is at the heart of this book, just as she was at the heart of the East London Federation of the Suffragettes, the following chapters will tell the story of the many other women (and some men) that formed this pioneering organisation.

Annie Kenney

Back in the early 1900s, Annie Kenney was one of the very few working-class women involved at the organising level of the WSPU. Annie was the fifth of eleven children, and began work in a cotton mill when she turned 10 in 1889. She worked from 6 a.m. to 12.30 p.m. until leaving school at the age of 13 and after that worked over 10 hours a day in the factory. It was gruelling and dangerous work: Annie even lost a finger when it was ripped off by a bobbin on one of the mill's spinning machines. She became involved in trade-union activities, sharing political newspapers, literature and poetry with her colleagues.

Annie first encountered Christabel Pankhurst at a meeting of the local branch of the Independent Labour Party and was captivated by her ideas. Her sister Jessie recalled the meeting, which she also attended, with another sister, Jane. Jessie commented that: 'Christabel said afterwards that three girls with shining eyes came up to her when she had spoken, and those three girls were us. Annie promised to work up a meeting for her. She got together all the factory girls and the meeting was a great success.' Annie joined the WSPU and organised more meetings. She began to speak at some meetings herself, and discovered a talent for making speeches, inspiring many with her unswerving commitment to the cause.

As Annie notes in her record, *Memories of a Militant*: 'The great difference between the old method and the new lay in the changing of a word. The old school said, "Are you in *favour* of women having the vote?" the new school said, "Will you *give* us the vote?"'

The militant phase of the women's suffrage movement is often said to have begun after 13 October 1905, when Annie and Christabel attended a Liberal Party public meeting and asked Winston Churchill and Sir Edward Grey, 'If you are elected, will you do your best to make women's suffrage a government measure?' They received no reply, and when they unfurled a 'Votes for Women' banner the pair were booed and thrown out of the hall. In the tussle which followed, a policeman claimed the women had kicked him. They were arrested, charged with assault, and sentenced to three days' imprisonment. Annie recalls the rally which was held on their release, again at the Free Trade Hall:

> It was just a week from our being boo'd out of the same hall. It was packed, and hundreds were turned away. Bouquets and flowers were given to us, songs of liberty were sung in our favour. Labour was in great prominence, vowing support, and cheering us to the echo. Christabel made a most eloquent speech, full of passion and fire. I delivered my speech, and I trembled as I made it. I felt nervous when I saw the great hall full of earnest, excited faces. I knew the change had come into my life. The old life had gone, a new life had come.

After her release from prison in 1905, Annie left her job at the factory, moved in with the Pankhursts and began working full time as a campaigner. It was Annie that Christabel and Emmeline charged with taking the work of the WSPU to London. Sylvia was already in London, but had not yet completed her scholarship at the Royal College of Art, so the task of mobilising the women of London was given to Annie.

The WSPU in East London

When she arrived in London in 1906, Annie stayed with Minnie Baldock in her home on Eclipse Street in Canning Town in West Ham, on the recommendation of socialist and feminist campaigner Dora Montefiore. Minnie knew women involved in all the different local groups and helped Annie to make contacts and find speaking engagements. The first London branch of the WSPU was opened in Canning Town that year, and swiftly followed by branches in Poplar, Bow, Stepney and Limehouse. In her memoirs, *Tough Annie*, Annie Barnes, then in her early twenties, recalls her first encounter with the Women's Social and Political Union when she saw a crowd of people trying to get into a meeting of 'Mrs Pankhurst's suffragettes' at the Edinburgh Castle pub, and police blocking them:

There was one policeman on horseback near a horse trough. Up and down in front of him wheeled a tall, posh lady in a wheel chair. Up and down she went and then she patted the horse. Somehow, she put her hand up under the stirrups, it wasn't clear just what she did, and the policeman went headfirst into the horse trough. Of course we all thought it was killing. But the police took hold of the woman in the wheel chair and put her in a van and took her to the police station … My goodness though, the police manhandled her! They were really shockingly brutal. Anyway the people in the end managed to get into the hall through the windows at the back and over the roof. This was all before I was involved in the fight for the vote.

It's quite possible that the 'posh lady in a wheelchair' that Annie admired was Rosa May Billinghurst, who joined the

WSPU in 1907. May suffered an illness as an infant that left her paralysed. Although she eventually regained the use of her upper body, she was never able to walk without crutches. She used a special tricycle wheelchair to get around, which was often decked out in the WSPU colours of purple, white and green, and in which she sometimes hid bricks to throw through windows. May was known for her enthusiasm, bravery and good sense of humour, which certainly fits with Annie's account.

Many women who would become prominent members of the East London Federation of the Suffragettes were members of these early WSPU branches. As well as Minnie Baldock, Annie Kenney and Sylvia met Daisy Parsons, who had worked in a cigarette factory in Aldgate, and who would later be part of the Federation's deputation to meet the Prime Minister, and would go on to become the first female mayor of West Ham.

They also met Adelaide Knight from Bethnal Green, a truly remarkable woman whose name has vanished from most popular accounts of the struggle for the vote, although in a 1906 letter her great friend Dora Montefiore refers to her as the 'leader' of the working women in the WSPU. After a severe illness as a child Adelaide used crutches for the rest of her life and endured repeatedly poor health. She was described as highly intelligent, with a love of poetry, music and history. In 1894 Adelaide married a black seaman, Donald Adolphus Brown, the same who was decorated for bravery by the King in 1921. He shared Adelaide's political beliefs – they both joined the Independent Labour Party and, in a step which many would find radical even today, he took Adelaide's surname and was widely known as Donald Knight.

Adelaide was secretary of the new WSPU branch in Canning Town in 1906, and in June that year, although her name was omitted from many of the press reports, she was arrested alongside Annie Kenney when they tried to gain an audience with Herbert Asquith. Donald looked after their two small children while she was imprisoned for six weeks for refusing to be 'bound over'. Adelaide wrote to him from prison, unrepentant: 'equal taxation demands equal representation, and I am determined to continue the fight for progress.'

Increasingly dismayed with the lack of democracy in the WSPU, Adelaide resigned as branch secretary in March 1907. The following year she was elected to the West Ham Board of Guardians where she served until 1910. Adelaide retained her socialist ideals and her friendship with Dora, and in 1920 they both became founding members of the Communist Party of Great Britain.

One of Annie and Sylvia's first actions in East London was to set about organising a march from Canning Town to Westminster, followed by a meeting. On learning of the plans, Emmeline Pankhurst was apparently dismayed. Caxton Hall, which Annie had booked for the meeting on the recommendation of Keir Hardie, was far larger than any other venue that the WSPU had used, and she feared that the new movement would look foolish. However, Emmeline agreed to speak anyway, and on the day – 16 February 1906 – the hall was filled with women of all classes who had come to hear her.

Several hundred women from East London were brought by train into Central London, where 'they unfurled a few simple banners, which were quickly furled again by the police' and marched to Westminster. There were women from many different backgrounds present. When it was announced that votes for women had not been mentioned in the King's Speech which was taking place that day, Emmeline Pankhurst commanded the audience to follow her to the House of Commons to lobby Members of Parliament, as Sylvia Pankhurst describes: 'she swayed her hearers as the harper commands his strings, and when she rose to march out through the rain, they followed her to a woman, though many of them had never set eyes on her before.'

However, on reaching the House of Commons they found their way was blocked by police. Thanks to the intervention of Keir Hardie and others, the women were eventually permitted to enter the lobby twenty at a time, the others waiting their turn in the torrential rain outside. Although the rain and cold was deeply unwelcome, it may have strengthened the movement in a small way:

> When, drenched and shivering, the women at last got speech with some Member of Parliament and found him indifferent, Mrs Pankhurst's appeal to their indignation was substantially reinforced. The opinion with which many of them had set out for the meeting, that the militant tactics were too aggressive to be justified, had begun to wane.

While the lobbying didn't move any politician's minds, the day secured widespread press coverage for the WSPU and brought in large numbers of new members. It was the first of many high-profile marches and rallies, of which most participants were working-class women from the East End, who dedicated their Sundays – for many their only day off in the week – to supporting the WSPU actions.

'Go on pestering'

The WSPU's next action in London was to attempt to meet with the Prime Minister, Sir Henry Campbell-Bannerman. After receiving no response to their official invitations, thirty women, including Annie Kenney, went to Downing Street and repeatedly rang the doorbell of Number 10 until they were arrested. Shortly afterwards, the prisoners were released and the WSPU received a message from the Prime Minister's office to say that he was prepared to meet with them. The meeting took place on 19 May 1906 in a crowded hall where over 250,000 women of various movements – including textile workers, students, socialists, temperance campaigners and many others – were represented by numerous delegates. One of whom was Emily Davies, one of the two women who had presented the first petition for women's suffrage to John Stuart Mill in 1866.

The Prime Minister replied at length, explaining that he agreed with their argument but 'was obliged to do nothing at all about it' and so urged the women to 'go on pestering' and to exercise 'the virtue of patience'. One of the oldest women present, Mrs Elmy, reminded the Prime Minister 'in her frail old voice' that she had been working for the women's suffrage cause since 1865. Then Annie Kenney 'jumped on a chair and shouted: "Sir, we are not satisfied! The agitation will go on!"' The next eight years were ones of disturbed peace, disrupted meetings, smashed glass, slashed paintings, burnt buildings, bloodshed and even lives lost. I wonder whether Campbell-Bannerman ever regretted his flippant words to this delegation in 1906. I hope so.

It was at this time that Charles Hands, writing in the *Daily Mail*, first described the WSPU's members as 'suffragettes', distinct from the non-militant or 'constitutional' suffragists. The women took up the label themselves with pride.

While poor women from the East End turned out in the greatest number for these early marches and meetings and attended many of those to follow, their place in the movement gradually shifted. Their enthusiasm and willingness to rally to the suffragette battle cry was viewed with increasing misgivings by Christabel Pankhurst. As early as 1906 she expressed her surprise that the WSPU should be exclusively dependent upon women of the East End during their mass protests. While she recognised this early and crucial participation, she simultaneously rejected their potential role in that struggle, which she saw as belonging to middle- and upper-class women. As the profile of the WSPU began to increase they started to attract wealthier and more respectable supporters, and the movement's base soon moved away from the East End.

Over the next year membership continued to grow; the headquarters moved to London from Manchester; two WSPU leaders, Frederick and Emmeline Pethick-Lawrence, launched a newspaper for the movement, called *Votes for Women*; and the Woman's Press was created, which oversaw publishing and printing for the organisation, marketing a variety of merchandise. In 1908 the WSPU adopted purple, white, and green as its official colours, chosen by Emmeline Pethick-Lawrence: 'Purple … stands for the royal blood that flows in the veins of every suffragette … white stands for purity in private and public life … green is the colour of hope and the emblem of spring.'

The Women's Social and Political Union continued to organise large-scale processions and rallies, including a 300,000-strong 'Women's Sunday' rally in Hyde Park in June 1908, as well as regular 'women's parliaments' which coincided with each new parliamentary session. Christabel Pankhurst stood trial for publishing a pamphlet that called on suffragettes to 'rush' the House of Commons, but skilfully used the situation to her advantage by conducting her own defence (she was a qualified lawyer) and putting Liberal ministers in the stand.

In 1908 the new Liberal Prime Minister, Herbert Asquith, declared his plans to extend the right to vote, but only to the men who were yet not on the electoral register. Increasingly frustrated at being told to be patient and wait their turn, WSPU members now began to throw stones and break the windows of government offices. The tactic of hunger striking among imprisoned WSPU demonstrators was also begun at this time, by Marion Wallace Dunlop, but in 1909 the government authorised the brutal practice of force-feeding hunger strikers.

When the Liberal government was re-elected in January 1910 a WSPU member, Jane Brailsford, and her journalist husband, Henry Brailsford, suggested a new idea: a private member Conciliation Bill which would unite parliamentary supporters of all parties. However, the bill would only enfranchise wealthy, property-owning women, a measure which meant that many would still be excluded. While this bill went before the House of Commons the WSPU declared a truce. The bill was voted through the second reading stage by 299 votes to 189, but was then blocked by Asquith, who stated that the government could give no further time to it, in that session or any other session. Shortly after this announcement, on 18 November 1910, 300 women arrived in Westminster to protest at the dropping of the bill, but they were met in Parliament Square by unprecedented violence from uniformed and plain-clothes police and some anti-suffragist demonstrators.

The day became known as 'Black Friday' because of the brutality with which the suffragettes were treated by the police and members of the crowd. There were witness reports of deliberate acts of cruelty and even sexual assault. Women were struck in the face and head and repeatedly knocked to the ground, and many were struck or grabbed by their breasts. The following week's *Votes for Women* newspaper reprinted a letter from a Mr C. Mansell-Moullin, Vice-President of the

Royal College of Surgeons, declaring his alarm at the injuries some of the women sustained:

> The women were treated with the greatest brutality. They were pushed about in all directions and thrown down by the police. Their arms were twisted until they were almost broken. Their thumbs were forcibly bent back, and they were tortured in other shameless ways that made one feel sick at the sight. I was there myself and saw many of these things done. The photographs that were published in the Press of November 19 prove it. And I have since seen the fearful bruises, showing the marks of the fingers, caused by the violence with which these women were treated.

As the government retaliated to the WSPU's actions with increasingly repressive measures and kept many of the movement's leaders under surveillance, the emphasis on individual acts of militancy became stronger, and the acts themselves more dramatic and dangerous.

Four

THE EAST LONDON FEDERATION OF THE SUFFRAGETTES

In 1912, persuaded largely by Sylvia Pankhurst, the Women's Social and Political Union (WSPU) decided to return to East London to campaign and recruit new members. Although for Sylvia the East End campaign represented a much more important opportunity:

> I regarded the rousing of the East End as of the utmost importance. My aim was not merely to make some members and establish some branches, but the larger task of bringing the district as a whole into a mass movement, from which only a few would stand aside ... The creation of a woman's movement in that great abyss of poverty would be a call and a rallying cry to the rise of similar movements in all parts of the country.

Although in her account Sylvia failed to acknowledge the area's existing women's movement, her sensitivity to the importance of working women claiming power for themselves – rather than playing a supporting role in a movement which had become dominated by the middle class – is plain to see:

I was anxious, too, to fortify the position of the working woman when the vote should actually be given; the existence of a strong, self-reliant movement amongst working women would be the greatest aid in safeguarding their rights in the days of settlement. Moreover, I was looking to the future; I wanted to rouse these women of the submerged mass to be, not merely the argument of more fortunate people, but to be fighters on their own account, despising mere platitudes and catch-cries, revolting against the hideous conditions about them, and demanding for themselves and their families a full share of the benefits of civilisation and progress.

The East End campaign

One October morning in 1912, Sylvia and her American friend Zelie Emerson set out down the 'dingy' Bow Road in search of suitable premises. They found an old baker's shop opposite St Mary's church, and 198 Bow Road became their campaign headquarters. Sylvia painted the board over the shop front with the words 'Votes for Women' in gold leaf, to the astonishment of the people of Bow. Another close friend and comrade of Sylvia's, Norah Smyth, took some striking photographs of Sylvia addressing the crowds from a wooden platform built with timber from the local Lansbury Wood Factory, donated by Willie Lansbury, the son of local MP George Lansbury.

We will hear more on the Lansbury family later. It's worth taking a moment to introduce Zelie Emerson and Norah Smyth, two friends of Sylvia's and both remarkable women in their own right (although they were often overshadowed by their charismatic friend). Both were deeply committed not just to the suffragette cause, but to the emancipation of working women, and abandoned status, comfort and wealth in order to advance it.

In her memoirs, Sylvia describes Zelie, originally from Michigan, as 'that merry little American, whose youthful desire for adventure had brought her across the Atlantic to join the movement', possessed of 'furious energy and resource'. It was Zelie's idea to create *The Woman's Dreadnought* newspaper for the Federation, and it was also because of Zelie that the organisation chose a base close to Roman Road. She was involved in all the Federation's various projects, but was also physically courageous, enduring hunger strike and force-feeding. On a number of occasions she sustained serious injuries through police brutality which damaged her health for many years to come.

Another name which occurs again and again at Sylvia's side is Norah Smyth. Although Norah was also from a wealthy background, she dedicated many years of her life, and almost all of her inheritance, to the suffragette cause, and lived in Bow with Sylvia for many years. Norah played a key role in all the Federation's activities (she was financial secretary, helped to drill the People's Army and even wallpapered and painted the Women's Hall) but seemed to prefer a place out of the limelight. Sylvia describes her as 'dogged in her fidelities, and by temperament unable to express herself under emotion'. Perhaps fittingly then, one of Norah's greatest contributions was as an observer. She had a talent for photography, and it is thanks to her that we have such a fantastic visual record of the East London suffragettes' activities, and so many images of the deep poverty which surrounded them.

From this base at Bow Road, the East London suffragettes organised their activities, delivering speeches and selling copies of the WSPU newspaper from the shop, in the street, and from a stall in the busy Roman Road market. The incomers were shocked by the deprivation they encountered, as Sylvia recalled in 1931:

> Women in sweated and unknown trades came to us telling their hardships: rope-makers, waste rubber cleaners, biscuit packers ... those who made wooden seeds to put in raspberry jam. Occupants of hideously unsavoury tenements asked us to visit and expose them. Hidden dwellings were revealed to us, so much built around them that many of their rooms were as dark as night all day ... I met a fragile orphan girl earning 7s a week and her food, minus 3d insurance, for washing up in a city restaurant until nine each night, and paying 6s a week in rent. It was 'hard to keep straight,' she said. I procured for her an offer of better work, but when I returned she was gone. I could find no trace. Her words haunted me.

While they quickly built up their support in the East End, with local women joining the WSPU in large numbers and their numerous meetings always well attended, the suffragettes encountered amusement, indifference and hostility. From 'urchins' pelting them with small stones, to grown men and women throwing fish heads and urine-soaked paper, to outright violence, the first few weeks of the campaign were challenging. However, all the speaking up was worth it, as their words carried over the 'filth and violence' to reach women like Annie Barnes:

> I'd never really thought about that sort of thing. I'd been very quietly brought up ... Then, one day, something happened which really woke me up ... there were four women on a cart speaking. That was unusual, to see women speaking.

> 'We want to do away with the sweatshops and all these terrible things that are happening ...' they were saying.

I said to mother, 'You go home, I'd like to listen.'

I listened to what each of the women had to say. The men in the crowd were just awful. They wouldn't listen and they just shouted at the women. Then I grasped what it was all about. The speakers were fighting for us women to have the vote ... At the end of the meeting the four women asked all those interested to leave their names and addresses ... Of course I went and gave my name and address ... I didn't tell my mother about it. I was a bit afraid. My parents would have died if they'd known I was involved, though they thought the suffragettes had a lot of pluck.

Shortly after Sylvia and Zelie set up their branch headquarters on Bow Road, the attention of the whole movement was suddenly focused on their new neighbourhood, following a surprising announcement by local MP George Lansbury.

George Lansbury

George Lansbury was born in Suffolk but his family moved to the East End when he was 9 years old. He left school at 14, working as a clerk, a grocer and in a coffee bar before starting his own business as a contractor. When the business failed, Lansbury and his young family emigrated to Australia, but didn't settle, so they soon returned to England and George began work at the timber merchants owned by his father-in-law. From then on he and his wife remained in Bow.

In 1886 Lansbury joined the Liberal Party. Annie Barnes, who became a Labour Councillor in Stepney in 1934, once asked him why he had decided to join the Labour Party instead. He told her that after joining the Liberals:

He went canvassing for elections in Devons Road, Bow, which was a very poor area. He told me how poor everyone was, how poorly dressed and badly nourished. He knocked on one door in Devons Road. He was young, full of beans, just starting out in politics. A woman came to the door. She had a sack over her, with a hole for her head and two for her arms. He could hardly believe his eyes. He was so shocked. When she understood what he'd come for she said, 'Canvassing! Do you expect us to bother about anything like that? Everything is in the pawnshop. We've got no money and we're starving.'

He was so struck that he couldn't say anything to her and he went away. He went home ... and got some money and some clothes. He went back to her and asked for the pawn tickets. 'You can have them, I've never been able to redeem things from there.' He went round to the pawnshop and ordered the things to be sent round to her. He'd never realised there was such poverty in the East End. After that he joined the Independent Labour Party and fought for the people. The Lansbury's made Poplar. They fought and fought, the whole family. .

In 1892, Lansbury was elected to the Poplar Board of Guardians. Lansbury and the rest of the Poplar Board used their position to improve conditions in the workhouse, including establishing a small farm in nearby Essex which provided work for the unemployed and taught the city dwellers how to grow and sell food.

Lansbury was elected as Labour MP for Bow & Bromley in 1910 and with Keir Hardie led the campaign in Parliament for women's suffrage. He once told the Liberal Prime Minister Herbert Asquith: 'You will go down in history as the man who tortured innocent women.' And so he has.

Lansbury's whole family became involved with the suffragette movement in East London: his daughter-in-law

Jessie was honorary secretary for the new East London branch of the WSPU and his sons Edgar and Willie provided timber from their business to build speaking platforms and furniture for the suffragettes' various projects. His daughters Annie, Dorothy, Daisy and Violet, daughter-in-law Minnie and wife Bessie were all involved in the East London Federation of the Suffragettes' activities. Their names appear in the records over and over again.

By 1912 George Lansbury was an influential figure in the Labour Party. On the advice of WSPU leader Christabel Pankhurst, he brought a resolution in support of women's suffrage to a Labour Party Conference. The resolution called for the party to oppose all government legislation until it introduced a bill which would give the vote to women. The idea behind the resolution was that the government would find it very difficult to pass any laws without the votes of the Labour MPs, and so this resolution would force them to prioritise women's suffrage.

Sylvia Pankhurst and Keir Hardie disagreed with this tactic, as they did not feel it would be effective, and also because, as Sylvia put it, 'that other overdue question of popular self-government, Home Rule for Ireland, to which the Labour Party was deeply pledged, was also in a critical and claimant position on the political stage.' Sylvia and Hardie both believed that the issue of whether Ireland should be allowed to govern itself was too important to ignore, but Christabel and Lansbury believed that an exclusive focus on the vote for women was the best strategy.

The resolution was defeated and Lansbury was told by the party that he must now fall into line or leave. He decided to leave, announcing that he would resign his seat in Parliament and stand for re-election as an independent candidate, with the votes for women at the heart of his manifesto.

As soon as the by-election was called, suffrage campaigners of all stripes arrived in Bow and Bromley and WSPU activity intensified. Additional resources, volunteers and materials poured into the constituency, with orders direct from the WSPU's leader Christabel Pankhurst, who was then based in Paris after seeking political refuge there. However, the election campaign was badly managed, as the WSPU and the local Labour activists who supported Lansbury failed to work together. At one event a Labour speaker stole a pitch which had been assigned to the WSPU. Lansbury's supporters were left to do the doorstep canvassing themselves without help from WSPU volunteers. Many Labour supporters were anti-suffrage, and heckled the WSPU speakers. Sylvia reported hearing a WSPU speaker railing against 'the men' at one open-air meeting – the men that they would shortly be relying on to vote Lansbury back into Parliament!

On election day Lansbury was defeated by the Conservative candidate by 731 votes. Following this disappointing result, word came from the WSPU headquarters, now at Lincoln's Inn Fields, to close down the East End campaign altogether. Sylvia protested, and managed to persuade her mother and sister to allow her to continue the work she had begun.

Shortly after George Lansbury's defeat, the remaining WSPU members and volunteers in East London organised a working women's deputation of twelve women to Lloyd George, drawn from all over the country but with most from the East End. These included: a Poplar laundress, a home-worker who made pinafores at sweated rates in Bow, a waste rubber worker from Poplar, and the wife of a labourer earning 22s a week, who had eight children and lived in a two-roomed tenement in Bethnal Green.

The deputation was scheduled for the day before some women's suffrage amendments to a Reform Bill were to be debated in Parliament. It was led by Flora Drummond, a skilled WSPU organiser who was nicknamed 'The General' after her habit of leading marches on horseback and wearing military-style uniform. Although Lloyd George assured the deputation that the amendments to the Reform Bill would be carried, the Speaker announced that same night that if this were done the whole Reform Bill would be out of order, and so the amendments would be dropped.

Sylvia was exasperated by the parliamentary machinations which seemed to block the movement at every turn, and angry at other campaigners' claims that there was no support for 'Womanhood Suffrage' (the vote for all adult women, with no qualifications of property or married status) which only strengthened her resolve to make sure working women had a voice within and beyond the movement. However, disappointed by this blow following so quickly from Lansbury's defeat, many of the West London suffragette volunteers and organisers abandoned the East End as a lost cause, and all financial aid to the various branches in the area were withdrawn. The shop at 198 Bow Road, too, was closed down.

The East London Federation of the Suffragettes

Determined to continue the movement's work in East London, Sylvia, Zelie, Norah and others encouraged local WSPU members to take on the roles left empty by 'imported officials', and so at the start of 1913 East London WSPU branches were to be found in Bow, Bromley, Stepney, Limehouse, Bethnal Green and Poplar, and the headquarters moved from the old baker's shop on Bow Road to Roman Road, after Zelie urged 'Come to the Roman Road; all the people go there!' Sylvia describes a lively, colourful street crammed with barrows 'laden with oranges, cabbages, garments, crockery and what not' and the way that a 'cheery kindliness held the throng, in spite of its poverty'. They found the only shop available to rent, number 321, which was not in the best state but which the landlord agreed to rent to them immediately:

> The shop window was broken across the centre and held together by putty, the flooring was in holes ... It had lately been a second-hand clothes dealer's and was bug-ridden, like many another East End hovel. Repeated fumigation and papering never entirely eradicated the pests. In spite of such drawbacks, the place was a centre of joyous enthusiasm. Mrs Wise, at the sweet shop next door, brought in a trestle table for a counter, and helped us to hoist the purple, white and green. Her boy volunteered to put up and take down the shutters night and morning; her girl came in to sweep. Friends rallied round; women of the neighbourhood scrubbed the floors and cleaned the windows; tables and chairs and crockery were given by poor people's self-denial.

On Monday, 17 February, a meeting was held at 'the obelisk', a memorial at the junction of Devons Road and High Street Bromley. Willie Lansbury, George's son, provided a wood cart for a platform and both Sylvia and Zelie addressed the crowd. It was a bitterly cold day, and Sylvia found that despite her rhetoric, the crowd was unenthusiastic. In desperation, she hurled a stone at the shop front of C. Selby, the undertaker, who had only recently opened his new premises on the corner. Sylvia succeeded in smashing a glass pane, and was promptly arrested. Not to be outdone, Willie broke a window in the Bromley Public Hall and Zelie raced down the road and smashed the window of the Liberal Club. They were arrested, along with Mrs Moore, Mrs Watkins and Annie Lansbury, and all were sentenced to a months' hard labour. The arrests sparked 'a tremendous flame of enthusiasm' for the movement in the East End. Supporters marched to Holloway eight times while the stone-throwers were incarcerated, and several times to Brixton, where Willie Lansbury was imprisoned.

Throughout the spring and summer of 1913 the suffragettes organised meetings and processions. Sylvia determined to speak on each occasion, although she risked arrest at every public appearance. One of the largest and most successful took place on Sunday, 25 May 1913: a Women's May Day procession. Members from the Bow, Bromley and Poplar branches spent many weeks in planning the event. Hundreds of branches were carried, decorated with pink almond blossoms made of paper, along with purple, white and green flags and the 'red caps of liberty'. With 'children in white with garlands of flowers, the great banners of the local Trade Union branches, and standards lettered by East End friends' it was 'the brightest show ever seen in the grey East End'. The procession started at the East India Dock Gates and concluded in Victoria Park, where fifteen platforms for speakers had been erected.

Following the success of this event, the various East London branches of the WSPU agreed to group together under the banner of the East London Federation of WSPU. The movement was thriving: 'the poor women of the slums were rushing to the movement as though all their life and all their hope depended upon it, spending in and for it every moment that could be snatched from their toil … a thousand members were quickly enrolled in the small district of North Bow alone.'

With the Federation's growing popularity and strength, Sylvia's increasing profile and independence and the WSPU's increasingly autocratic leadership and focus on wealthy West London, there were tensions which came to a head at the end of 1913. After Sylvia spoke publicly in favour of Home Rule for Ireland, she received a letter from her sister Christabel summoning her to Paris.

On their arrival in Paris in January 1914, Sylvia and Norah found a chilly reception. They were curtly informed by Christabel that the new East London Federation of the WSPU must become a separate organisation. On enquiring the reason for this, Sylvia and Norah were told that it had become necessary as Sylvia was 'mixed up with' other organisations and causes. Christabel explained: 'You have your own ideas. We do not want that; we want all our women to take their instructions and walk in step like an army!' In addition:

> ... a working women's movement was of no value: working women were the weakest portion of the sex: how could it be otherwise? Their lives were too hard, their education too meagre to equip them for the contest. 'Surely it is a mistake to use the weakest for the struggle! We want picked women, the very strongest and most intelligent'.

This is taken from Sylvia's account, written some years later, and so should perhaps be taken with a pinch of salt. However, Edwardian England was a place of rigid class divisions and intense prejudice, and Christabel's views would not have been out of step with most of her contemporaries.

Back in London the news was met with indignation from the Federation's committee, though they knew there were fundamental differences in approach. The minutes from this meeting record the observation that: 'We had more faith in what could be done by stirring up working women ... where they had most faith in what could be done for the vote by people of means and influence. In other words that they were working from the top down and we from the bottom up.'

The committee voted to change their name slightly to become the East London Federation of the Suffragettes, to the great annoyance of Mrs Pankhurst. In the first issue of the Federation's new newspaper, *The Woman's Dreadnought*, published on 8 March (International Women's Day!) 1914, their tone is defiant: 'Some people say that the lives of working women are too hard and their education too small for them to become a powerful voice in winning the vote. Such people have forgotten their history.'

Over the next few years the Federation did prove the power of a working women's movement. Their influence and importance extended far beyond their impact on the struggle for Votes for Women, and they became an independent force for change in the East End.

Five

PROTEST, POLICE AND THE PEOPLE'S ARMY

Protest, peaceful or otherwise, was central to the work of the East London Federation of the Suffragettes in all its various incarnations. Alongside their other activities a huge number of demonstrations, rallies and processions were held over the years. While many were festive occasions, with music and activities for children, many were met with violence from police and crowds. However, as the Federation became more and more rooted in the communities around Bow, Canning Town, Poplar and Bromley their processions were joined by huge numbers of supporters, many of whom were men, as this report from *The Christian Commonwealth* newspaper on 15 July 1914 shows:

> Quite half the audience were men, vocal and emphatic in their approval of the aims of the meeting – all types of men, but chiefly workers, many of them socialist and trade unionists, and the majority of them rather rebellious about orthodox politics.

Rather rebellious

During the struggle to win the vote women were routinely arrested for peaceful as well as militant protest. Between 1905 and 1914 over 1,000 suffragettes were imprisoned. For many this was their first experience of arrest or imprisonment, but far from deterring them there are countless examples of women whose resolve was strengthened by their treatment at the hands of the law.

In June 1906, for instance, Annie Kenney was arrested during a demonstration outside the house of Herbert Asquith, then Chancellor of the Exchequer. The magistrate sentenced her to six weeks in prison for refusing to be bound over to keep the peace. Afterwards she wrote:

> He does not know himself, perhaps, how much he has done for me. He could not have sent me to a better school. If he had wished to brand the wrong done to women on my memory, if he had wished to forge my will in the furnace of hot indignation, and send me forth determined as never before to fight on to the finish, he could not have chosen a better way to do it.

A letter from Melvina Walker, written from Holloway Prison to her 'comrades in Limehouse' which was published in *The Woman's Dreadnought* in March 1914 expresses a similar sentiment:

> They have sent me here thinking they will break my spirit and that the punishment which they have inflicted on me will make me give up asking for the vote. No, friends, they have given me an experience which I would not give up for twenty pounds! I shall come out of this place with a greater desire to fight for the Cause to the bitter end …

The arrests, ill-treatment and heavy sentences faced by suffragettes not only galvanised the individual women that endured them, but built a feeling of solidarity within the movement, and a powerful sense of protectiveness towards its leaders. Another report from the *Dreadnought* records the warning of Mary Paterson following her court appearance:

> ... it took ten men and eight horses to arrest me ... You incite to breach of the peace when you give seven years to Julia Decies [a young woman who shot and wounded her lover after he treated her appallingly] and also drag people like Sylvia Pankhurst back again to prison. You have roused a fire in the East End and ten men and eight horses won't be enough next time!

Force-feeding

While she was imprisoned in Holloway in February 1913, Sylvia was force-fed for the first time while on hunger strike. During the next few turbulent months, many of the militant suffragettes were arrested several times, and during each spell of imprisonment they undertook a hunger and thirst strike. The aim was to destroy their health to the extent that they would be released to continue agitation.

The practice of force-feeding was approved for use on hunger strikers by Asquith's government in 1909; it had previously only been used in medical cases to save life. Although the three Liberal Home Secretaries in post during the time that force-feeding was widely used – Herbert Gladstone, Winston Churchill and Reginald McKenna – claimed that there was no associated pain or danger, it is now widely recognised to have been a brutal practice. Sylvia Pankhurst's description is shocking even today:

There were six of them, all much bigger and stronger than I. They flung me on my back on the bed, and held me down firmly by shoulders and wrists, hips, knees and ankles ... My eyes were shut ... A man's hands were trying to force open my mouth ... His fingers were striving to pull my lips apart – getting inside. I felt them and a steel instrument pressing round my gums, feeling for gaps in my teeth ... A steel instrument pressed my gums, cutting into the flesh ... A stab of sharp, intolerable agony. I wrenched my head free. Again they grasped me. Again the struggle ... Then something gradually forced my jaws apart as a screw was turned; the pain was like having the teeth drawn. They were trying to get the tube down my throat, I was struggling madly to stiffen my muscles and close my throat. They got it down, I suppose, though I was unconscious of anything then save a mad revolt of struggling, for they said at last: 'That's all!' and I vomited as the tube came up.

Those who had been force-fed often experienced acute mental distress alongside the physical symptoms, and there is another harrowing passage in Sylvia's 1931 book *The Suffragette Movement* about an event which occurred when Sylvia and Zelie Emerson were both on hunger strike in Holloway, and had been force-fed daily for some weeks:

That evening an officer came to fetch me to Zelie Emerson's cell. She was ill and asking for me. They hoped that I might quiet her. I knew by the dry, burning touch of her skin that she had fever. She complained of terrible abdominal pain. Shocked at her condition, I took her in my arms, uttering foolish words: 'Oh, my little sweetheart! Oh, my little sweetheart!' Her wrist was bandaged. She told me she had tried to commit suicide by cutting an artery. She had dug into the flesh with her small, blunt penknife, till she reached the artery, but when she had tried to cut it, she found it, she said, too tough, and like an India-rubber band. They had come to the cell while she was working at it.

This heartbreaking scene provides a stark contrast with the many jolly jokes, cartoons and caricatures produced at the time which ridiculed the suffragettes. Even now, the women who fought for the right to vote do not always receive the respect due to civil rights activists and political prisoners who underwent torture and state-sanctioned violence in their fight to secure something which we take for granted today. In the same year as Zelie's suicide attempt, Emily Wilding Davison stepped out in front of the King's horse at the Epsom Derby, and died shortly afterwards from her injuries. She had also previously attempted suicide in prison, after being force-fed.

There was a public outcry about the use of the practice, and many high-profile figures, including Keir Hardie, George Bernard Shaw and others, campaigned against it. In August 1912, a group of medical professionals published a report in *The Lancet* which condemned forcible feeding as a form of torture:

It has been stated by the Home Secretary that the practice of forcible feeding is unattended by danger or pain. We have carefully considered the written statements of 102 of the suffrage prisoners, of whom 90 have been subjected to the operation of forcible feeding; we have personally examined a large number of these prisoners after their release, and we have communicated with the physicians who have attended those prisoners whose condition on release necessitated medical care ... We are confident that were the details of the statements we have read and the cases we have examined fully known to the profession, this practice, which consists in fact of a severe physical and mental torture, could no longer be carried out in prisons of the twentieth century.

Each time Sylvia was released from prison, weak and exhausted from her hunger strike and the effects of force-feeding, she was lovingly nursed back to health by Mrs Jessie Payne, 'a dark, pale woman, of middle age, with one of the most benevolent faces I have ever known' at her home in 28 Ford Road, Bow. Jessie and her husband, both shoemakers by trade, lived in a two-roomed tenement and one can only imagine their sacrifice in having to give up one of their rooms to Sylvia. Once Sylvia had been released detectives asked at every house on Ford Road whether they could hire a room for their surveillance purposes, but at every house they were refused.

Jump, Sylvia!

After the introduction of the Prisoners (Temporary Discharge for Ill Health) Act, more commonly known as the 'Cat and Mouse Act', in April 1913, it became even more difficult for Sylvia to speak in public as she almost always faced re-arrest. For several months the police chased her around countless meetings and gatherings, where she was defended by the Federation's supporters, frequently leading to scuffles between the audience and the police which sometimes turned violent.

One particularly violent incident took place in Bow Baths Hall in October 1913. Sylvia had hidden in the Lansbury's house in St Stephen's Road; she then entered the hall in disguise. The people held the door back against the detectives trying to get in, but plain-clothes policemen sprang on to the platform on which Sylvia was speaking from behind the curtains. Annie Barnes was present at this meeting and described what happened next in her book *Tough Annie*:

> Suddenly, people in the audience started shouting 'Jump, Sylvia, jump, jump'. And they picked her up and threw her this way and that way among the crowd, changing hats with her so that the police didn't know which one she was. Goodness, it was exciting! Then as the police were in force outside the building, on foot and on horseback, one of Sylvia's aides put the fire hydrant out the window and aimed it at the police. The horses reared and in the commotion Sylvia escaped, and dashed around the corner where Willie Lansbury, George Lansbury's son, was waiting with a wood cart.

When Sylvia jumped from the stage she saw policemen smashing chairs and striking people in the audience. Mrs Mary Leigh was knocked unconscious; Mrs Ives was held up by the collar and struck with a truncheon, which broke her arm. Miss Forbes Robertson, sister of the great actor Johnston Forbes Robertson, also had her arm broken. Many other men and women were injured in the melee. As Zelie Emerson was leaving the hall, a detective, enraged by her calls of 'Puss, Puss' – a reference to the Cat and Mouse Act – struck out at her, hitting the side of her head. Mr Mansell-Moullin, the surgeon at the London Hospital who examined her, stated that if the blow had been struck an eighth of an inch further back she would have been killed. Her skull had in fact been fractured, and in the months after this incident Zelie was plagued by headaches and sickness and ordered to rest. In May the following year she returned to America. The *Dreadnought* records that 'Several members of the E.L.F.S and two American friends, who waved the Stars and Stripes, were at Waterloo to show our appreciation of the splendid fight that Miss Emerson has made for the international freedom of women'.

The next night, Sylvia spoke at Poplar Town Hall, and was promptly arrested. John and Jennie McKay, who were later both Poplar Councillors, rushed to her aid and were also arrested. On her release nine days later, Sylvia had to be carried on a stretcher to Bow Baths Hall and Poplar Town Hall to fulfil her speaking engagements. On 5 November 1913, another meeting was held in Bow Baths. Sylvia first went to the Lansbury's house in St Stephen's Road. The house was immediately surrounded by detectives, who mistakenly arrested Daisy Lansbury as she emerged wearing Sylvia's hat and coat. By the time they had discovered their error, Sylvia was in the hall addressing the crowds.

As a result of the above disturbances, Poplar Borough Council decided to withdraw permission for the suffragettes to hold their meetings in Poplar Town Hall, Bow Baths and Bromley Public Hall. In response Zelie Emerson organised a protest meeting at the Bow Palace on 14 December 1913. After the meeting she led a procession to the home of Councillor John Le Manquais in Tomlin's Grove. The procession, which was mostly women and children, was led by the band of the Gas Workers' Trade Union. On reaching Tomlin's Grove they found that the street's gas lamps had been extinguished, and they were immediately surrounded by mounted police, who attacked them. Here is the report from the *Manchester Guardian*:

> The shouts of police officers directing their men to clear the streets were mingled with the yells of women and children, who rushed here and there to seek safety. The main body of processionists rushed helter-skelter up and down the street in front of the mounted police, shrieking wildly and frantically

at their pursuers. Women and children were thrown to the ground in the melee, many being trampled on in the semi-darkness ... The majority of the processionists sought an exit into Bow Road, and here they were followed by a detachment of mounted police, who speedily broke up any formation there was in their ranks ... The street ... was excessively crowded when the procession entered it. On one side runs a blank wall, and there was no shelter for women and children except in the houses on the opposite side of the street.

Several members of the procession, the band and a few passers-by were seriously injured, including five children. Nine people were arrested, but were later released by the magistrate. Sylvia believed that 'The police were taking their revenge for many defeats; they had often done the same to break the spirit of the people in trade disputes'.

In one week in May 1914 there were two more shocking incidences of brutality against suffragette demonstrations. Mrs Emmeline Pankhurst put out an appeal to all women suffragettes to attend a march to Buckingham Palace to petition the King on 21 May. Many did but were met with force by the police. Daisy Parsons, a member of the East London Federation of the Suffragettes, was there and her description of what she saw was printed in the following week's edition of *The Woman's Dreadnought*:

Mrs Parsons entered the park by Admiralty Arch, and made her way to the Victoria Memorial. There she saw a large crowd of people, a large proportion of whom were youths hardly out of their teens, standing with their backs to the memorial, watching the palace. There was a wide vacant space between the people and the palace, and the middle of this space was a line of police, not standing shoulder to shoulder but with a space of some yards between each one ... Every now and then a woman would dart out from amongst the dense throng of spectators into the space, and the police rushed at her, caught her, and threw her back into the crowd. Then the young men in the crowd would turn on the woman and beat her and tear her clothes and drag down her hair and shout that she ought to be burnt. Then the woman would run out again towards the police only to be caught and thrown back again by the police and again beaten by the men. This would be repeated until at last she was hustled away out of sight or placed under arrest. In one case Mrs Parsons saw one woman face this eleven times before arrest. The police never attempted to protect any of the women who were assaulted, and one young woman they lifted right up and threw over the heads of the nearest people.

At last the mounted police came up at a gallop and drove everyone away ... She saw a young woman dressed in pink with a jeering crowd behind her. The young woman stopped and stood with her back against the wall. A sentry walked up to her and pushed her. She said 'How dare you', and he struck her in the face with his fist.

Another ELFS member, Charlotte Drake, was there with May Billinghurst in her wheelchair, who drove directly at the police with typical daring:

I was beside her. They threw us back, but we returned. Two policemen picked up the tricycle with Miss Billinghurst in it, turned it over, and dropped her on the ground. The excitement gave me strength – I picked her up bodily and lifted her back. We straightened the machine as best we could, rested a little to take breath and struggled on again. The police would not

take us – only knock us about. Then in the enormous crowd
I got sent flying one way and, she another. I tried to find her.
It seemed as though the earth had swallowed her …

A few days later, on 24 May and back in East London, the
Federation held its second Women's May Day celebration in
Victoria Park. To try and prevent Sylvia from being recaptured
by the police under the Cat and Mouse Act, twenty men and
women formed a chained guard around Sylvia Pankhurst.
They wore belts around their waists and were chained
together in a square, with Sylvia in the centre. As the chained
guard reached the park gates, they were surrounded by police
who dragged them into the boating enclosure, where they
smashed the padlocks with their truncheons and arrested
Sylvia. The procession broke up in confusion and several
fights took place between the police and those determined to
defend the suffragettes.

In a bid to protect themselves against the police and anti-
suffrage crowds, towards the end of 1913 the suffragettes
organised a 'People's Army', inspired by James Connolly's
Irish Citizen's Army which had been formed in 1913 during
an industrial dispute. The idea behind the Citizen's Army was
to give the locked-out men a chance to defend themselves
in clashes with the police, as well as maintain solidarity and
routine while the men were unemployed. The People's Army
was less militaristic, and aimed to be 'an organization men
and women may join in order to fight for freedom. And in
order that they might fit themselves to cope with the brutality
of government servants.'

Sylvia had no desire for the suffragettes' clashes with the
police to become any more violent, but in *The Suffragette
Movement* she remembers the unique political context:
'Yet with militancy springing up on every hand, it seemed then

that we were on the eve of great social changes and contests. I knew not whither the future might lead us. For the present I saw that our movement was awakening masses of women, and men also, to a strong desire for better conditions. I saw that the police now shrank from attacking us in the East End; I wanted that shrinking accentuated.'

Men and women were trained in the art of self-defence, and were drilled in Victoria Park, with the help of Sir Francis Vane, an unusual character who was on the one hand a hereditary peer and an army major, but on the other a peace campaigner and a supporter of women's suffrage, with socialist and republican sympathies. Vane, who was also involved in the early days of the Scouting movement, drafted the following pledge for the People's Army recruits:

> I promise to serve the common cause of Justice and my comrades under our duly elected Officers. I will be a friend to all and a brother to every member of the People's Army. I am a sincere believer in a Vote for every woman and every man.

The People's Army was evidently still in force in February 1914, when they were being drilled on Roman Road by Norah Smyth, beating a big bass drum. The police turned out in large numbers to break up the drill and Norah Smyth was arrested and brought before the magistrate on the charge of kicking a policeman on the right ankle and hitting him on the back of his neck with her drum stick.

The Great Procession

One of the biggest processions organised by the East London Federation of the Suffragettes took place early in June 1914, after Sylvia Pankhurst had written to Prime Minister

Herbert Asquith requesting, and then demanding, that he meet with a deputation of working women from the East End to hear their case for the vote. If he did not agree to meet them, she pledged to hunger strike to the point of death, and vowed that she would die on the steps of the House of Commons. Of course, Asquith refused.

On 10 June thousands of the Federation's members and supporters gathered in Bow for a procession to Westminster, accompanying Sylvia, who had to be carried in a chair as she was too weak to walk, and the elected deputation. The sight was described by Henry W. Nevison in *The Woman's Dreadnought*:

> It was eight o'clock on Wednesday evening. The whole of Old Ford Road, far away on both sides of No. 400, was packed with working people ... They had gathered straight from their work. Many had not been home to wash or eat ... It means something for hard-worked people to march five miles to Westminster and five miles back, to risk arrest or injury, loss of work and poverty for their families. Thousands took the risk ... We passed along the south side of Victoria Park. Every window was crammed with people. So were the pavements ... A religious silence prevailed. Again all took off their hats and many cried.

It came as no surprise at all that the march had only moved a few streets away from its starting point before the police attacked, wrenching the poles of Sylvia's chair out of the hands of those carrying it and knocking them to the floor. Sylvia was carried to a waiting taxi and taken back to Holloway to finish her sentence under the Cat and Mouse Act. The plan was to continue the procession:

The band played again, and with cheers we entered Mile End Road. Right up it we marched, our numbers continually growing. Past the People's Palace, past the London Hospital … The sight going down Ludgate Hill was very remarkable. The East India Dock contingent with Lansbury and Scurr had joined us then. The procession stretched right from the Old Bailey half way up the opposite hill of Fleet Street …

When the procession arrived at Westminster, Nevison accompanied the deputation of women into the Lobby, which was:

… filled with Members and strangers who had come expecting to see savages and were taken aback when they saw intelligent human beings. They evidently thought that when Miss Sylvia Pankhurst was arrested the crowd would disperse and the deputation would go sadly home. But they did not reckon on the earnestness of purpose that fills the people of East London, nor realize how vital to them is this matter of their enfranchisement. A really popular movement exists, and nothing will deter the women from accomplishing their purpose.

The deputation was told that the Prime Minister was unavailable by a Mr Illingworth, who went on to say that he had already received many deputations about women's suffrage, to which the women replied: 'Not of our class, and we are as important as others. In fact we are the people who keep you all.'

The procession did go home, but not sadly. The following morning plans for a campaign to secure a meeting with Asquith – and in so doing save Sylvia's life – were drawn up and put into action, as East London Federation of the Suffragettes member Mary Paterson described in *The Woman's Dreadnought*:

Meetings of members were held in each of the districts, at which volunteers came forward eagerly for every kind of work that was needed. The instant their day's work was over, working women and men set off to interview their Member of Parliament at the House of Commons, to urge them to do all they could to get Mr Asquith to yield. This work was kept up every day until the end, and Mr Asquith, Mr McKenna and other M.P.s were bombarded with letters and postcards to the same effect.

Then, for the younger members especially, there was poster-parading, bill distribution, and *Dreadnought* selling. There was the picketing outside Holloway, to wait for the release of our dear prisoner – day and night – by day, in two-hour stretches; by night, for all night at once; we took our turns at this sentry duty. Our young factory-girl workers cheerfully devoted the only leisure of their busy week to work of one kind or another. The married women, as cheerfully, and by dint of getting up earlier and carefully planning their work, took their share of all.

Just over a week after the procession on 18 June, Sylvia was released, so weak from her hunger strike that she could not walk or even stand, and taken from Holloway back to the House of Commons in a taxi. 'The saddest sight and one of the cruellest that one could see in a lifetime, was when she was lifted out of the car, too ill to help herself in any way, and laid down on the steps at the Strangers' Entrance,' Mrs Watkins wrote in the *Dreadnought*:

Inspector Rogers informed her that she would not be able to stay there: she told him she would wait until Mr Asquith consented to receive the deputation. Just as the police were about to drag her away, Mr Lansbury came out, and it would be impossible to describe the joy we felt on hearing that the Prime Minister had given in by promising to receive six working women at 11 o'clock on Saturday morning. How we all cheered, and with what joy we went home, knowing, for a time at least, the life we all value so much was to be spared, and the terrible torture for that night at any rate, was over.

The news was met with huge relief in the East End, followed by celebration and excitement: it felt like a turning point.

The deputation to Downing Street

On the morning of Saturday, 20 June a deputation of six East End women arrived at 10 Downing Street to make their voices heard. The deputation, which had been elected at three large meetings in Canning Town, Poplar and Bow, was led by Mrs Julia Scurr, who had been campaigning for women's suffrage in East London for many years, and consisted of: Mrs Payne, Mrs Bird, Mrs Ford, Mrs 'Hughes' and Mrs Parsons.

Mrs Scurr began the meeting by delivering a speech which Sylvia had helped to write, listing some of the most pressing problems facing working women, and calling for the opportunity to help solve them by participation in law-making:

Parliament is constantly dealing also with questions affecting the education and care of our children, with the houses in which we live, and more and more with every item of our daily lives. We feel ... that it is both unwise and unjust to legislate without the help of women ... We would further point out that whilst women are taxed on exactly the same basis as men; and like men are obliged to obey the same laws, they are allowed no voice in these questions.

We women of East London are much concerned in regard to social conditions in our district. There is very great poverty around us and the rents are terribly high. There is much unemployment amongst the men and a very large proportion of the women are the principal breadwinners, although they are both the childbearers and the keepers of the home. We want to say to you that, in our view, a woman attending to her home is as much a wage earner as if she went out into a factory, and that because women bring children into the world they perform the greatest of all services to the State, and they have the greatest of all reasons to desire to help in securing its welfare.

Mrs 'Hughes' spoke first after Mrs Scurr's introduction. Her name was actually Mrs Savoy: she used a pseudonym because her husband objected to having his name in the papers. George Lansbury called Mrs Savoy 'the best woman in Old Ford,' as in spite of her poverty and ill health she was jolly, brave and generous: 'she was bringing up two orphan boys, and was ever ready to share her last crust, or perform any service for a neighbour, from bringing her baby into the world to scrubbing out her room, or minding her children at need.' Her speech to the Prime Minister was brief, but effectively communicated the hardship she had known her whole life:

I am a brush maker, and I work from eight in the morning till six at night making brushes ten hours a day, and while I work I have to cut my hands with wire, as the bristles are very soft to get in. I have brought brushes to show to you. This is a brush I have to make for 2d, and it is worth 10s 6d. (Mrs Hughes then walked to the table and laid a brush and a bundle of bristles on it. The Prime Minister and the officials who were present started nervously as though they feared that the brush might be a bomb.) …

As I have to work so hard to support myself I think it is very wrong that I cannot have a voice in the making of the laws that I have to uphold … I do not like having to work 14 hours a day without having a voice on it, and I think when a woman works 14 hours a day she has a right to a vote, as her husband has … We want votes for women.

Mrs Hughes' point was echoed by Mrs Ford, who explained that she had started work in a jam factory at 11 years old: 'I do think, as we have to work under those conditions, we should be the ones who should be able to bring forward reforms, and help to voice them and show what is really wanted in the reform of sweated labour.'

Mrs Ford also attacked the sexual double standard, using a tragic story of a young friend of hers as an illustration of the impossible situation for unmarried mothers:

She had to go to the Workhouse to have a baby. When she came out she had no mother and no home to go to. I took her with me, and she shared my bed and my room, where there was five of us. Money was very short, and sooner than take the food, as she felt she was doing, out of my children's mouths … she went away, and I did not see her until three days afterwards when she was drawn out of the river Lea with her child.

Next spoke Mrs Daisy Parsons:

I left school at 12 years of age and had a delicate father, and a mother who had to work hard at washing and charring. I had very often to help the neighbours do their work for which I was paid sixpence a day and the little food they could give which was not very much, because people in the East End do not have much food to give away. On the other spare days I used to help at home with the younger brothers while mother was at work. Then after a little while I went to work in a factory in Aldgate and there I was a cigarette packer. We used to pack a thousand cigarettes for 3d and in the morning when we were quite fresh we could pack 2000 cigarettes, but as we got tired after dinner we could only pack a thousand and a half. There you see that the wages some days that we earned were less than a shilling a day. In that factory the men were allowed time for lunch simply because they were men, but the women and girls, if we were fortunate enough to have lunch and could take bread and butter with us, had not a place to eat our lunch and were forced to take it into the lavatory and we know that is not altogether the thing. The men could quite openly come along with cans and eat whatever they liked to send out for and sit and eat it at their leisure. We know that if the men were working under these conditions, through their trade unions, and through their votes they would say they would not tolerate that sort of thing.

Mrs Bird and Mrs Payne spoke next. Having listened to all six women's speeches and asked a few questions, Asquith – a vocal opponent of women's suffrage – delivered an uncharacteristically sympathetic response:

I will take all these things into careful consideration ... On one point I am glad to say I am in complete agreement with you ... if you are going to give the franchise to women, you must give it to them upon the same terms that you do to men. That is, make it a democratic measure. It is no good tinkering with a thing of this kind ... If the change has to come, we must face it boldly and make it thoroughgoing and democratic in its basis.

This last comment was received with hope and optimism by the members and supporters of the East London Federation of the Suffragettes, by the rest of the movement and by the press: the *Manchester Guardian* wrote that the deputation's speeches highlighted 'the average poor woman's argument for enfranchisement and the average rich man's argument against it', and Asquith's reply was viewed as of 'most happy augury'. *The New Statesman* suggested that the Prime Minister's reception of this deputation 'marks a distinct step forward in the Suffrage agitation' and *The Nation* believed it could be 'a new departure and a new chapter of hope in the history of this question'.

Six

SPREADING THE WORD

The East London Federation of the Suffragettes understood that getting their message out was essential to raising awareness, and to recruiting and mobilising the women of the East End, but before radio, television or the internet this was no mean feat. Billboard advertising was expensive then as it is now, and besides, they were radicals – it's likely that many companies selling advertising space would not have wanted to do business with a group of militants. They printed posters, handbills and pamphlets, they wrote and were written about in newspapers, but that still didn't allow them to reach the large numbers of East End people at that time who were unable to read. Through their constant, impassioned public speaking, and by developing ingenious ways to harness the most powerful communications tool of all – word of mouth – the Federation succeeded in reaching many thousands of women and men with its call for equality and justice.

Speaking out

East London has a long tradition of public speaking, open-air rallies and lively political meetings, which continues to the present day. At the start of the twentieth century, with widespread illiteracy, and limited access to free newspapers (which didn't much concern themselves with the views and interests of working people anyway), free public meetings were a vital source of news and information. Listening to speeches became a common pastime even among people who weren't necessarily involved in any particular cause. Stepney suffragette Annie Barnes remembers first encountering the suffragettes by chance at a local pub: 'There was a big hall there that was used for big meetings. You never knew who was going to hire it. I think the Salvation Army hired it sometimes and they gave the kids buns and cups of cocoa. Anyway, out of curiosity, I walked down just to see what was going on.'

When they arrived in the East End, the Women's Social and Political Union took full advantage of this tradition and the existing network of venues and audiences. With the help of local activists like Minnie Baldock, speakers including Sylvia and Annie Kenney recruited new WSPU members by speaking as widely as possible. One of the great assets of the suffragette movement was its pool of fiery, inspiring, passionate speakers. In particular Emmeline, Christabel and Sylvia Pankhurst were in great demand, and acted as a huge draw at any meeting. Annie Barnes remembered: 'We used to chalk the pavements advertising meetings. "COME AND HEAR SYLVIA PANKHURST AT SO AND SO". And the crowds used to come.'

One of the differences that was to emerge between the WSPU's approach to campaigning and that of the Federation centred on who was encouraged, or even permitted, to speak. The WSPU ultimately became a very autocratic organisation, with a tightly controlled 'party line' and a number of high profile speakers who could be relied upon to stay 'on-message'. In many ways this was a very effective tactic, as Emmeline and Christabel Pankhurst built a powerful unity and consistency across the whole of their campaign.

However, this inevitably created a focus on individual 'stars' which Sylvia found very uncomfortable, even as a star speaker herself. And whether because of differences in education, or because of outright prejudice, most of the stars of the WSPU were middle- or upper-class women. Sometimes they spoke on behalf of working-class women. More often they forgot. Sylvia was more interested in building a mass movement in which working women were empowered to speak for themselves. And even in the very early days of the WSPU's East End campaign in 1912, the East London suffragettes were claiming their right to be heard – a group of local suffragettes, led by Melvina Walker, demanded that there should be at least one speaker from the local branch on every platform.

With a tremendous talent for public speaking, Melvina Walker was to become one of the most popular speakers in London, among any movement. 'She seemed to me like a woman of the French Revolution,' Sylvia observed in *The Home Front*: 'I could imagine her on the barricades, waving the bonnet rouge, urging on the fighters with impassioned cries. When in full flood of her oratory, she appeared the very embodiment of toiling, famine-ridden, proletarian womanhood.' Melvina lived in Poplar where she was married to a docker, but previously she had been a lady's maid, an experience which gave her a cool confidence around her 'betters', having seen what went on behind the scenes in their great houses. She had 'black eyes, feline in their mysterious aloofness and uncertainty, blazing at times with a swift and sudden fire'.

Members of the Federation were encouraged to speak in public, at meetings, at open-air rallies, at their weekly stall at Roman Road market, or even just on the street. Many, like Melvina Walker, discovered a natural talent for it; others attended the inexpensive speaking classes advertised in the *Dreadnought*: 'Miss Amy Hicks M.A. Will take a Speakers' Class at 20 Railway Street, Poplar, on Monday evenings, at 8pm, beginning April 26th. The course will consist of twelve lessons. The fee will be 1s which may be paid in 1d instalments.'

As well as speaking about the suffrage cause in the East End, many of the women accompanied Sylvia to other events, including WSPU branch meetings in places like Kensington and Mayfair, where their speeches made a powerful impression on their wealthy audiences.

In its early years, the East London Federation of the Suffragettes sent several deputations of working women to meet politicians and ministers in Westminster. The membership of these delegations was decided democratically, through votes at large public meetings. While many of the women who made up these delegations were confident and accomplished political speakers who could advance a case for their cause – whether votes for women, wartime price controls or old age pensions – the transcripts of these meetings show that they continually referred to their own life and experiences, and those of people they knew. In her memoirs, Sylvia Pankhurst more than once refers to Melvina Walker's 'tales of woe', and the effect they made on listening crowds. As well as campaigners, the members of the Federation were clearly positioning themselves as what we might now call 'experts by experience', which gave them an authority that their class and gender denied them.

A number of members of the East London Federation of the Suffragettes went on to be active in local politics, as campaigners, councillors and even mayors, in the case of Daisy Parsons, Nellie Cressall and Dorothy Lansbury. 'Tough' Annie Barnes was a Labour Councillor in Stepney from 1934 to 1948 and always credited her famous confidence to her experience as a suffragette: 'Being in the suffragettes did a lot for me. I couldn't say "Boo" to a goose before that. It really brought me out.'

One instance of this confidence in action is recorded in Annie's memoirs. On the eve of the 1921 general election, the local Conservative Party held a meeting in Limehouse Town Hall for their new candidate, Evan Morgan. Annie and her brother went along and listened as the new candidate was introduced as a 'very handsome fellow'. The fellow went on to promise that he would eradicate unemployment in Limehouse, whereby Annie stood up to speak and refused to wait until the end. The audience started calling for her to be heard and the candidate invited her up to the platform, to show he was a gentleman. Annie began:

'Friends', I said, 'our candidate here, oh yes, he's a perfect gentleman. I'm not disputing that. His father's a coal owner, Lord Tredegar. He's shut down the mines in South Wales and opened up in India because he could get people to work out there for next to nothing ... and the miners, our miners, are out of work. If this gentleman is so concerned about the Limehouse people, why does he do nothing to relieve his father's unemployed in South Wales?

People started to say, 'Well yes, she's right.' Well, it was logic, wasn't it? I went on.

'He comes to Limehouse. What does he know about us? If he gets in tomorrow you won't see him again. He'll enjoy being a Member of Parliament, but if he had any real concern for the people he'd do something about the miners who are out of work.'

Well, he hadn't expected all that. There was a commotion. They wouldn't listen to him any more. They had to get the police in to escort him out. He never had time to answer.

Everyone was shouting 'She's right, she's right.' I never said anything if I wasn't sure I was right. Sylvia had taught me that. I got all that courage from being in the suffragettes.

The Woman's Dreadnought

'I want you to start a paper,' Zelie Emerson told Sylvia Pankhurst in January 1914, shortly after the East London Federation of the Suffragettes formally split from the Women's Social and Political Union (WSPU). As the Federation was no longer guaranteed space in the WSPU's newspaper, *The Suffragette*, which at any rate 'gave little attention' to the concerns and cares of working women, it became clear that they needed a mouthpiece of their own.

Though Sylvia would be editor and chief writer of their new newspaper, it was Zelie who got the project off the ground – consulting printers, producing dummy sheets, deciding the size and format and securing a small amount of advertising (for Neave's baby food and Lipton's cocoa). Federation members chose *The Woman's Dreadnought* as the title at a general meeting, although Sylvia later said she would have preferred 'The Worker's Mate'. They agreed that the paper would be sold for a halfpenny for the first four days; any leftover copies would then be distributed for free. An advance copy was published on International Women's Day, 8 March 1914, and explained itself thus:

> The name of our paper, *The Woman's Dreadnought*, is symbolic of the fact that the women who are fighting for freedom must fear nothing ... the chief duty of *The Dreadnought* will be to deal with the franchise question from the working woman's point of view, and to report the activities of the votes for women movement in East London.

From the next issue on 21 March, the *Dreadnought* was produced weekly until July 1924. In 1917 its name was changed to *The Worker's Dreadnought*, and over its decade-long existence its focus expanded to include national and international politics, war, peace and revolution. In its first few months, 20,000 copies were printed each week, but the circulation was reduced to 10,000 after the outbreak of war when the cost of paper rose sharply. Sylvia Pankhurst wasn't the first female newspaper editor – Rachel Sassoon Beer and Mary Howarth came before her – but she was a pioneer in a field which is dominated by men even today, 100 years later.

As well as providing a channel for the Federation to reach current and potential members in the East End with their campaign messages, the paper quickly took on an important role as a platform for the voices of working women and men to be heard and as a way to draw attention to injustices. In *The Suffragette Movement*, Sylvia wrote:

> It was my earnest desire that it should be a medium through which working women, however unlettered, might express themselves, and find their interests defended ... I wanted the paper to be as far as possible written from life; no dry arguments, but a vivid presentment of things as they are,

arguing always from the particular, with all its human features, to the general principle ... Our volunteer working women reporters, when investigating conditions, produced far truer accounts than any Fleet Street journalist, for they knew what to ask and how to win the confidence of the sufferers.

It is the work of these reporters that makes the paper so remarkable, then and now. As well as giving the reader a very rich picture of the activities of the Federation itself – there are notices about jumble sales, clothing exchanges, a suffragette choir, a discounted illustration course, calls for donations of books, reports from branch meetings and countless other titbits – the *Dreadnought* is one of the few publications from this era in which it is possible to hear the voices of working-class women. The following excerpt comes from a 1915 article, one of many first-hand accounts of the work and conditions in East End factories which was published in the *Dreadnought*. Florence Buchan worked at the jam factory of Messrs. James Keiller & Sons in Silvertown:

The jam pots and glasses are washed on brushes, and the girls are always getting their hands cut, and having to have them bandaged up. It is very awkward for them to work with rags on their hands. Very often a girl gets a piece of glass or china in her hand which causes inflammation, and she has to have it lanced. Jam pot washing is very dirty work, and girls have to stand in pools of water and get their skirts and ankles very wet. Clogs are supplied but they fit badly and are very loose at the ankles, so that the wet gets inside and the irons underneath often cause the girls to slip on the wet stones and sometimes they are badly hurt.

Girls must be 18 when they start in the preserving department and we have to take our chance of getting regular work as there are the busy and slack seasons. There are the marmalade season and the jam seasons. The jam is a very busy time, especially when the strawberries are in. We are paid 1 d or 1 ¼ d per basket according to the strawberries. It is impossible for the employees to pick all the stalks and bad berries out if they are to make enough to live on at those rates. Girls sit on boxes, four at a tub and as they pick they put the fruit in the tub, and the stalks on the floor. Then men take the strawberries away to be 'pulped', that is put in a large pan and all mixed up together with any of last year's jam that is left.

When machines were brought in to attach parchment lids to the jars of jam and wrap them in paper, Florence lost her job, along with some other, newer girls. When Florence asked their boss why she had got the sack despite having worked in the factory for two years he implied that it was because of her involvement with the suffragettes, a reminder of the price that some women had to pay for their part in the movement.

In another article, from May 1914, Melvina Walker (describing herself as 'a docker's wife') reports on a day spent knocking on doors in one of the poorest areas of East London to invite women to attend a suffragette meeting, and to learn more about their thoughts on the campaign for women's suffrage. This canvassing is standard practice for political parties, but not many are brave enough to publish what they hear on the doorstep:

✳ A tall, thin, poorly clad woman came to the door, the wife of a casual labourer, with a baby at her breast. Did not know anything at all about women's suffrage; never did any reading; very seldom went out; never did any shopping, because the little shop across the road gave her 'tick' and so she had to keep going to them. Her husband came into the passage;

he looked as if he could do with a meal more a day. He had been out of work for weeks.

✻ Woman was too busy all day to go to meetings. She looked very poor, and when asked if she would like to come to the evening meetings, said that she was too tired, and that she was glad when the children were in bed so that she could sit down in the chair and close her eyes for a rest.

✻ Woman, yes, had heard about it; couldn't see the use of the vote: if we had to work as hard as she, we wouldn't have time for votes. She had six children going to school, and had to do the needlework as well. She came to the door with a pair of trousers that she was 'finishing' in her hand.

✻ A woman thought it was time something was done for women. She thought the Insurance Act a robbery. She was sure that if the women got into Parliament they would manage things better than that. Asked what she thought of the Housing question, thought it was disgraceful. Things as they are 'don't give you any heart to clean. Good luck to you, hope you get the vote.'

✻ Mother of nine children, said she had gone through something in her time, but gloried in the pluck of the Suffragette, wished she was younger, would be out with them. Of course she thought women should have the vote, and thought that the reason why men didn't want us to have it, was because they wanted all their own way. 'I wouldn't have no man dictate to me, a mother of nine children,' and she drew herself up in a dignified manner, 'I believe in holding my own.' Her husband often calls her a suffragette. She says 'you flatter me when you call me that, for those women have got pluck!'

✻ Woman said, men have always voted and what good have they done? She thought woman's lot was a hard one, and, 'if you think us getting the vote will alter it, then it *will* be a God send!'

* Woman thought the men had the best time of it: 'it's true they have to work and earn the few ha pence they get, but when they dub off on Friday, they think they're giving you a fortune: 23 shillings mine gives me and four babies to keep, and in the middle of the week they come on you for a sub and if you haven't any money they ask you what you've done with it all, and then they start on you. It's a hard life and I stand at 5s rent, what can you do? Do you know what? I would rather he'd stick to the few ha'pence, and *he* keep the home, but there, *he couldn't do it*! Men have got no worry, women have it all.'

* Mother of seven children, asked if she would come to the meeting, said she would ask her husband.

* Woman complained that landlord must have his rent every Monday, but that she could not get him to do anything in the place. It was always cleaning but never clean. 'It doesn't give you any heart!' She would come to the meetings, for she had very little pleasure. Husband out of work.

* Refined looking woman came to door; house quite a nice appearance, top half of house to let. Said she had five children, and believed that when women were in power, they would alter things ... She complained of the cost of living – 'things were getting worse and worse.' She made a stew every day of the week for the children, except Sunday, because she thought it the cheapest, and 'you can't make stew without onions, and believe me they are asking 3d a pound for them.' She did not think life was worth living, but must put up with it for the sake of the children.

At the end of the list, Mrs Walker includes a summary of 'Lessons to be learned', the first of which is to refute the government's view of housewives as 'unoccupied'. She lists the key issues that came up: 'unemployed problem ... Poverty – Housing Question – Women as Slaves – Sweating of Women

– Insurance Act a failure', but ends on the optimistic note: 'Suffragettes to be found in slums.'

The *Dreadnought* had an awareness-raising function beyond the subject of votes for women, as a brief item addressed 'To Sweated Women' shows:

The Trade Boards Act, which gives the Local Government Board power to set up Boards for fixing minimum wages, applies to the following trades:

1 – Ready-made and wholesale bespoke tailoring
2 – Box making in paper, cardboard, chip or similar material
3 – Machine made lace and net
4 – Hammered and dollied or tommied chain making
5 – Sugar (confectionary and food-preserving)
6 – Shirt making
7 – Hollow-ware making (including the making of tin vases and canisters)
8 – Linen and cotton embroidery

Women who work in any of these trades or on any Government contract work should communicate with us if they are paid at sweated rates.

For women working in the very worst conditions and for the lowest pay, who were generally not members of a union, and who often worked from home at night, isolated from any camaraderie which could be found in the factories, information about their rights was not easily available. In the *Dreadnought* they could learn what they were entitled to, and also read stories of women who had claimed their rights and more, usually through industrial action but occasionally through the newspaper's intervention. This was the case for the workers at Lusty's Turtle Soup Company of Salmon Lane, Limehouse. A small item appeared in one issue, describing the grim conditions of work at the soup factory:

> Wages are 10s a week or 2d an hour, and 2d an hour overtime. The basement in which the women work is wet and steaming. In one morning 24 women plucked and cleaned 500 fowls, some of which they said were alive with maggots. It is whispered that these fowls were to be sent to the troops at the front.

A few weeks later another item appeared: 'We are glad to state that as a result of our exposure of the conditions at Lusty's Soup Co. at Poplar, 1s a week rise has been given to the women.' But typically for the Federation, they weren't prepared to leave it at that: 'This is a paltry increase. We look for more and have informed the War Office of what happens at Lusty's.'

But the *Dreadnought* wasn't all news, it featured speeches, cartoons, letters and poems which all worked to raise awareness of injustice and inspire working women and men to take action. Some of the letters and poems in particular are reminiscent of the 'consciousness-raising' groups and literature of the 1970s women's liberation movement. There is a clear urge to relate the demands and values of the Federation to the everyday experience of working women, as these extracts from a poem by Martha Watt reveal:

> To cook and wash and sew, that's all my lot
> It's all I can do, day in day out
> As time runs into weeks and months and years
> That's all my life, there isn't any more …

> But thoughts all melting gold flash in my brain …

Just foolish thoughts that go and leave me cold
The world's soon real again and work comes round,
Suppers to get and washing-up to do
And children's Sunday clothes to put away,
Just foolish thoughts that make my poor heart long
Just foolish thoughts, but yet why should it be?

Almost fifty years before Betty Friedan's *The Feminine Mystique*, the boredom, frustration and loneliness experienced by many housewives is articulated here, and was no doubt recognised by many of the *Dreadnought*'s readers.

Where did those readers come from? One of the central activities of the members of the East London Federation of the Suffragettes was selling the *Dreadnought*, taking it to factories at closing time, to markets and pubs. This wasn't just an effective way to get the word out but a simple, practical way that women could contribute to the movement. As Annie Barnes recalls, 'I had commitments at home looking after all my brothers and sisters, I couldn't chance imprisonment. But I did volunteer for things that were less risky.' Annie used to deliver copies of the paper:

> … round and about. My father didn't know anything about this. I'm sure he wouldn't have approved at all as he had a business. Mrs Moore used to bring the newspapers to the side entrance. After the children were in bed, I used to slip out and deliver them. The old man didn't know where I was. Not that he took any interest anyway in anything we did.

A special badge in the Federation's colours – white, purple, green and red – was awarded to members who sold more than 1,000 copies of the *Dreadnought*, and they received a public acknowledgement in the paper. Congratulations Mrs Schlette,

Mrs Payne, Mrs Parsons, Mrs Millo, Miss O'Brien, Mrs Crabb, Mrs Bird and Miss Marks! Members were encouraged to put up posters, leave copies in libraries, and sell them to newsagents – even to buy gift subscriptions for their friends and family.

The *Dreadnought* was not only groundbreaking because it had a woman editor, and because it was dedicated to sharing the views and words of working-class women, but also because it maintained an unusual balance of very local news and notices and an international outlook. On one page the reader finds a report from a demonstration in Bromley, on the next an article about suffragists in Hungary and another one about the first woman to be made a Justice of the Peace in the USA. In marked contrast, the Women's Social and Political Union paper, *The Suffragette*, was relaunched as *Britannia*, and took a fervently pro-war, nationalist line.

Sylvia, as editor, hired the UK's first black journalist, Claude McKay, in 1920. McKay had arrived in London from the USA in autumn 1919 and met a number of left-leaning public figures at the International Socialist Club. In 1920 George Lansbury's socialist newspaper *The Daily Herald* published a deeply racist article written by E.D. Morel, entitled 'Black Scourge in Europe: Sexual Horror Let Loose by France on the Rhine'. Outraged, McKay penned a response, which Lansbury refused to print. Sylvia, however, offered to print it in *The Worker's Dreadnought*. After this, Sylvia invited McKay to become a regular paid writer for the paper. Later, he recalled:

> Sylvia Pankhurst wrote asking me to call at her printing office in Fleet Street. I found a plain little Queen Victoria sized woman with plenty of long unruly bronze-like hair. There was no distinction about her clothes, and on the whole she was very undistinguished. But her eyes were fiery, even a little fanatic, with a glint of shrewdness.

She said she wanted me to do some work for the *Workers' Dreadnought*. Perhaps I could dig up something along the London docks from the coloured as well as the white seaman and write from a point of view which would be fresh and different. Also I was assigned to read the foreign newspapers from America, India, Australia, and other parts of the British Empire, and mark the items which might interest *Dreadnought* readers.

In the same year Sylvia was arrested and imprisoned for five months for sedition – inciting insurrection against the established order – after publishing a number of anti-war articles in the *Dreadnought*. McKay's rooms were also searched as part of the investigation. Later McKay lived in Russia and then the USA, becoming a successful author of novels, short stories and poems.

Women's Halls

The opening of the first Women's Hall at 400 Old Ford Road in May 1914 was a significant event. It established a permanent base for the East London Federation of the Suffragettes, and for the next ten years was Sylvia's home in the East End. The hall was opened on 5 May, which was Sylvia's 32nd birthday, and a celebration was held in her honour. The occasion was reported by an E. Haverfield in *The Woman's Dreadnought*, under the title 'Our House Warming':

A very pleasant evening was spent by members and friends of the ELFS on May 5th, to celebrate Miss Sylvia Pankhurst's birthday by the opening of a large hall attached to her future residence. The pleasantest part of the whole affair to this writer was the love and esteem in which Sylvia is held by her friends in the East End, who presented her with a handsome fitted dress case, a beautiful hair brush made by Mrs Savoy, the member who gave it and innumerable others ...

The hall had been painted by men supporters [and Norah!] who had given up the previous Saturday afternoon to the work. The forms had been stained by the members of the Federation. Excellent refreshments, all made by members, were served. There was much merry conversation, and informally at a late hour this pleasant evening drew to a close.

As well as a house in which Sylvia, Norah Smyth and Mr and Mrs Payne were to live, the premises contained a large hall, holding about 350 people and a smaller hall which could hold about fifty or sixty people. Again Sylvia turned to the Lansbury's for help, and Willie and Edgar supplied the wood to make tables and benches.

The symbolic importance of a permanent 'home' for the East London Federation of the Suffragettes was matched by its practical importance for their operations and in particular for getting the word out about their campaigns. With a large hall of their own, the suffragettes were able to hold public meetings without fear of interference from the council or the police. Other sympathetic groups could hold their meetings there too, bringing in a new audience for the Federation's messages and building solidarity with other campaigns in the East End at the time. Without having to pay hire fees, the Federation could run a much wider range of activities, including lessons and workshops, fundraising concerts, lending libraries, affordable canteens and nurseries.

It also meant that everyone in the community knew where to go to find Sylvia, and to ask for help from the suffragettes.

The *Dreadnought* and Sylvia's memoirs record countless people who arrived, desperate, at the door of 400 Old Ford Road. Whether in need of information, representation, employment, medical help or simply a way to feed their children, many hundreds of people turned to the suffragettes, knowing that they would find assistance without the stigma of charity. In the years following 1914 several other women's centres were established, one on the corner of Old Ford Road and St Stephen's Road in Bow, another at 20 Railway Street in Poplar and another at 53 St Leonard's Street in Bromley.

The East London Federation of the Suffragettes placed women's self-representation at the heart of their work. Rather than simply distributing crude propaganda, the Federation created numerous innovative ways for the local community to connect with and take ownership of their movement.

1 Keir Hardie. (Courtesy of the Library of Congress, LC-DIG-ggbain-01224)

Above 2 Emmeline Pankhurst. (Courtesy of the Library of Congress, LC-USZ62-87662)

Right 3 Sylvia Pankhurst at Ford Road, by Norah Smyth. (The International Institute of Social History)

Left 4 'Tough' Annie Barnes.

Below 5 Bow Children, by Norah Smyth. All the images which follow were also taken by Norah. (The International Institute of Social History)

Right 6 A sleeping child in Bow, 1915. (The International Institute of Social History)

Below 7 Another photograph by Norah, this time showing the ELFS Procession passing Bow Bus Station in June 1914. (The International Institute of Social History)

8 Norah Smyth, Sylvia and Zelie Emerson. (The International Institute of Social History)

9 Sylvia recovering from hunger strike in 1913. (The International Institute of Social History)

NORAH L. SMYTH   SYLVIA PANKHURST   BARBARA TCHAYKOVSKY, M.D.

MISS BALCHIN   MRS. DRAKE   MRS. PAGE
MRS. PASCOE   MRS. MANTLE   MRS. PARSONS
MRS. JESSIE LANSBURY   MRS. McCHEYNE

10 ELFS
committee,
from the
Dreadnought.

11 Deputation to 10 Downing Street in June 1914. (The International Institute of Social History)

12 The Roman Road stall.
(The International Institute of Social History)

13 Melvina Walker and Nellie Cressall.
(The International Institute of Social History)

14 Trafalgar Square anti-conscription rally. (The International Institute of Social History)

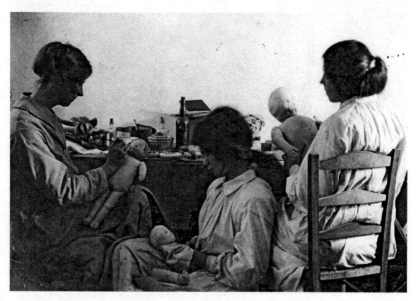

15 Toy Factory at Bow. (The International Institute of Social History)

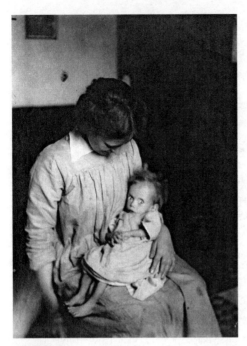

16 Nurse Hebbes with a malnourished child in 1915. (The International Institute of Social History)

17 The ELFS with their nursery in 1914. (The International Institute of Social History)

18 Cost price restaurant. (The International Institute of Social History)

19 Another view of the cost price restaurant. (The International Institute of Social History)

20 Junior Suffragettes Club in Victoria Park. (The International Institute of Social History)

21 New Year Pageant in 1916. (The International Institute of Social History)

22 Rose Pengelly leading the strikers. (The International Institute of Social History)

23 Pageant in Victoria Park. (The International Institute of Social History)

24 The much-loved George Lansbury, the rebellious Mayor of Bow.
(Courtesy of the Library of Congress, LC-DIG-ggbain-36844)

Seven

THE WAR

In June 1914, while the East London Federation of the Suffragettes were still celebrating the success of their meeting with Prime Minister Herbert Asquith at 10 Downing Street, and Sylvia was recovering from her latest hunger strike, the clouds of war were gathering in Europe. On 28 June, Archduke Franz Ferdinand, heir to the Austro-Hungarian Empire, was assassinated by a nationalist group in Serbia. One month later, Austria-Hungary declared war on Serbia, igniting a tangled web of alliances around Europe. Germany, Russia, Montenegro, France and Belgium were pulled into the war, and on 4 August, Britain joined too when she declared war on Germany.

While the idea of the 'home front' is more strongly associated with the Second than the First World War, the impact of the war was felt deeply and immediately. While air raids by German zeppelins and biplanes wrought physical destruction, the war brought about devastating social and economic effects in the poorest parts of the country, including the East End.

Unlike the Women's Social and Political Union (WSPU) and the National Union of Women's Suffrage Societies (NUWSS), the East London Federation of the Suffragettes did not give up their campaign for women's right to vote during the war. And while the other two organisations threw themselves into the war effort with a ferocious nationalism, the Federation took on war work of a different kind. Despite Sylvia's deeply held anti-militarism and her belief that the war was set to be an imperialist bloodbath, the Federation did not adopt an explicit anti-war stance until 1916. This was partly because the full horror of the war was yet to unfold, and also because virtually everyone in the community had a son, brother, husband or father who had enlisted. Instead, in the first few months of the conflict the Federation conducted a huge relief programme in East London, helping the hardest hit to fight off starvation.

The war was to shape their work for the next four years. Even as early as January 1915, this advert for a public meeting features a long list of issues connected to the war (although 'Votes for Women' still tops the bill):

Keep the Votes for Women flag flying!

Come to demand Votes for Women now!

Come to stand up for the Soldier's wife and mother.

Demand the abolition of police supervision [of women receiving an army allowance] and pensions of £1 a week for the mother and 5s a week for each child.

Come to protest against State regulation of vice. Remember Josephine Butler. Has she lived in vain?

Come to demand work for those who are unemployed through the War!

Come to demand a living wage of 5d an hour for women employed on all work subsidised by Government funds, or working for Government contractors.

Come to demand for women a voice in averting the horrors of war, and in bringing all wars to an end.

Come to demand a Vote for every woman over 21!

Hunger on the home front

Within a few weeks of the outbreak of war many East End factories had closed. Workers had no benefits to fall back on and little chance of finding another position. Unemployment rose dramatically, and the Federation found itself facing hundreds of cases of deep poverty and starvation, many of which were printed in summary in *The Woman's Dreadnought*. Here are some typical examples selected from pages and pages of similar stories:

Mrs B. – Coat finisher, very little work since war began … Husband casual labourer earning 15s a week, out of work six weeks, cannot get a job because of war. Six children, ages four months to eleven years. Rent 4s for two rooms.

Mrs B. – Five young children, expecting another any day, two children have dinner at school. Husband dock labourer out of work through war. Landlord has given notice to quit. Pawned everything and now starving.

Mrs F. – Young widow with two children, one and a half and three and a half years. Parish allows 7s a week … Works at home making children's underclothing, gets 4d for a dozen petticoats. No work now on account of war.

Two girls living near Victoria Park, employed in making caramels four and a half and five years at the same firm and earning from 10s to 12s per week, are now thrown out of employment through the war.

Mrs H has four children, aged 15 months, four, eight and nine years. Husband waterside labourer, work very slack. Baby very

ill with pneumonia the last two weeks, still very bad. Rent 4s 6d
per week. Have promised milk while baby is so bad.

As men on the Army reserves list were called up and others
enlisted, many women were suddenly left alone to provide
for their family, sometimes with just a few hours' notice.
In her book *The Home Front*, Sylvia Pankhurst wrote about
the numerous cases which were brought to her in the early
months of the war. Here's just one example:

> A woman stopped me in the Old Ford Road to tell her trouble.
> Her man had been taken for the War, with only three hours'
> respite to say good-bye. He had served his time in the Army
> before she knew him, and until the calling-up notice came, she
> had never realised what his being a Reservist might someday
> mean. He had given her 10 shillings when he went away, and
> told her to make it last as long as she could. It was all spent
> now; no more money had come from any source, and she could
> get no work – her voice failed in a sob. As we spoke together
> her two little boys ran up to her. They had the wilted look I saw
> growing upon the children; they seemed like fading flowers.

With only antiquated Poor Laws, the workhouse, and minimal
National Insurance coverage in place of a welfare state, within
weeks of war's outbreak many families in the East End were
facing starvation. While separation allowances to provide for
soldiers' wives and children were slowly introduced, they were
not generous, were often paid late and could be suspended for
weeks at a time. The queues at town halls all over the country
were enormous, and marriage and birth certificates requested
as proof cost money to acquire, and were frequently lost by
the administration. One of the members of the East London
Federation of the Suffragettes, Mrs Murray of Canning Town,

was denied all support when the War Office failed to return her marriage certificate in the post. She wrote to Sylvia:

> I think it is a shame that the Government should be allowed to do such things just because you are poor ... When they take your man you might as well say they have took all you possess; and they don't care so long as they have him, what becomes of them left behind.

Similar problems were encountered as the war took its bloody toll and more and more women were left as widows, not only grieving for lost husbands, fathers, brothers, sons and friends, but struggling to access the allowance that would allow them to feed their children and themselves. Even when they could access the allowance, it often didn't cover their basic needs, as an example printed in *The Woman's Dreadnought* in December 1914 shows. The article includes the meagre weekly budget of 'Mrs S. of Poplar' who 'has five children and is expecting another'. With rent, bread, coal, meat, vegetables, margarine, tea, sugar, milk and soap it comes to £1 10s 1d, but the allowance she received as a soldier's wife was just 27s 6d a week. 'She has pawned all she can, and is in debt ... She expects her husband home for Christmas, and does not know where his Christmas dinner is to come from.' The article then launches into a demand for better treatment, and relates the predicament of Mrs S. back to women's lack of political representation:

> We demand that the minimum naval or military pension should be £1 a week for the mother and 5s a week for each child. Pensions to be granted as a right, not a charity ... Soldiers' and sailors' wives should at once form an association to voice their demands and to protect their interests. If only they could

form an association of voters, they could easily safeguard their position. Like other women, they need the vote!

Every day in the early months of the war people arrived at the suffragettes' Women's Hall seeking help, some in desperate need, seriously ill, facing homelessness or on the brink of starvation. While Sylvia and the rest of the Federation were always clear that their work in the East End was not about charity – it was about building a strong, mass movement of working women who could and would demand their rights – the sheer scale of the suffering triggered by the outbreak of war forced them to adopt new strategies. One of their first initiatives came about almost by accident, when they received notice that a supporter was bringing milk from the countryside to help feed infants in need. News spread quickly, and soon hundreds of women stood in the street outside the hall with their children. Sadly, when the lady arrived she had brought just a few pints of milk, and almost all the infants went away still hungry. Jessie Payne was shocked by the want revealed by this misunderstanding, and suggested that the Federation could do something to help. Sylvia wrote a letter to *The Times* calling for donations and they soon began to receive money to buy milk, which they began to distribute from the Women's Hall.

Soon further milk distribution centres were opened in Canning Town, Stepney and Poplar. But this was just the start of the Federation's war-relief activities. They soon opened a clinic to treat the children worst affected by hunger and disease, an employment bureau, a nursery where women could leave their children safely while they went out to work, and three canteens serving nutritious food at 'cost price', anticipating the government's National Kitchens by several years. The suffragettes even opened a co-operative toy factory, where local women could earn a living wage and learn a trade at the same time.

War work

However, the Federation wanted to offer more than 'the bitter bread of charity', and continuously lobbied the government for measures to reduce the impact of the war on poor households. They took issue with some charitable efforts which they believed contributed to the unemployment crisis. The most prominent of these targets was Queen Mary's Needlework Guild, who launched an energetic drive to produce garments for soldiers. Although apparently rather shy, Queen Mary was 'a charitable bulldozer', and during the war 'she became a one-woman co-ordinating body for the administration of wartime charity', according to the *Oxford Dictionary of National Biography*. Shortly after the guild drive began, *The Woman's Dreadnought* featured a special appeal to wealthy women *not* to take up their sewing baskets:

> Prevention of distress by the keeping down of prices, so that the people are able to pay for the things they need, and by the provision of employment at a fair rate of pay is by far the best means of helping those who are themselves thrown out of employment by the war or whose breadwinners are withdrawn … We would put forward a very special appeal to leisured people not to start sewing for the soldiers and others whilst women who hitherto have earned their bread by such tasks are left to starve.

Although she is unlikely to have been a *Dreadnought* reader, the Queen seems to have been considering the same problem. Soon after Needlework Guild branches up and down the country began their furious muffler-making, the Queen's Work for Women Fund was created to provide employment for women who had lost their income through the war. The Fund set up an office at 88 Portland Place and there 'gathered together numbers of capable women busy all day long in the work of organizing', as Jennie Randolph Churchill (mother of Winston Churchill) put it. In her 1916 book, *Women's War Work*, Churchill gives a patronising but well-meaning account of its activities:

> No woman is turned away unheard, unhelped or unfed. To the seamstress and milliner, sewing is handed to be done at Trade Union rates. Typists, actresses, tea-shop girls, and any other worker who has lost her occupation through the war, can apply and be sure of help.

> 'I 'ardly 'ad the nerve to go,' said a young girl who had been on the variety stage in a troupe of acrobats, 'For I couldn't do anything useful. But they smiled at me ever so kind, and one lady in furs sez, "Oh, we wants such as you to learn." So I felt all right after that.'

> The directors asked her in which direction her fancies lay, and she chose to be taught the mysteries of toy-making with excellent results. Other women are anxious to learn the domesticated arts, cooking, washing, and laundering; while some hanker after open-air employment, and find a new joy in life out in the country, in working on the land, in some cases fruit-farming, in others devoting their time to nursery-garden work.

> But wherever the occupation is new, the women and girls are 'paid to learn.' Three pence an hour is given with good meals and expert tuition! It reads like a fairy tale to the woman at close grips with real poverty, but it is sound common-sense and national economy. It means that the mothers of the next generation can become capable, dependable women —

women who can train their families worthily and well, while those on the Fund who do not marry will find the benefit of this training as workers in the future. Married or single, these trained women must prove a strength to their country long after the War is finished ...

One of the triumphs of the Queen's Work for Women Fund is that its band of organizers make everything clear as daylight to the women who have to be helped. No matter if a girl be stupid, helpless even — for all the applicants have not had equal educational advantages — there is always kindly patience ready, always a friendly desire to explain and to aid. The Work for Women Fund exhibits clearly the genius of the educated woman, who is quick to seize upon possible opportunities and to point the way to others of her sex less fortunately placed.

The Queen found an unlikely ally for her new project in Mary MacArthur, founder of the National Federation of Women Workers and secretary of the Women's Trade Union League, who became Secretary of the Fund. MacArthur's appointment was initially welcomed by Sylvia Pankhurst, as MacArthur 'had a great reputation as a pioneer organiser of trade unionism for women, and as a propagandist against sweating'. Her hopes were dashed as it was announced that the Queen's Workrooms would pay just 10s a week, and for girls aged between 16 and 18 just 5s a week. The numerous household budgets submitted to the *Dreadnought* show that it would be virtually impossible for a woman to support even a small family on this sum alone, and even if she received an allowance for a husband or son in the services it would be a struggle to feed her children and pay the rent. Sylvia christened the workrooms 'Queen Mary's Sweatshops', and although they were closed in February 1915 she felt the damage was done, as 'they had set the common standard for women's war relief wages organised under other auspices, and they undoubtedly contributed towards riveting sweated wages on the women who were flocking into all branches of industry to replace men'.

In the coming years and months many factories reopened under government contracts, producing munitions, supplies or clothes for the Army. As more and more men went to the front, women began working in these factories in ever greater numbers. Of course poor women have always worked, and there are numerous examples of women in the East End working in dangerous, heavy, physically demanding jobs well before the war began. But this was one of the first times that women were brought in specifically to take up roles formerly reserved for men, although naturally they were paid less than a man's wages, and many were working in sweated conditions.

At the same time that many found themselves suddenly out of work, prices for food, cloth and other goods began to spiral. During the early months of the war this was largely due to panic buying. In autumn 1914, Sylvia led a deputation of Federation members to see Walter Runciman, President of the Board of Trade, to argue for food price controls. The party included Melvina Walker and Jessie Payne, as well as Charlotte Drake, 'a fair Saxon type, bleached by the hardships of an East End mother, clear-eyed in serene tenderness for her children, with a unique bluntness of racy utterance, always decisive', 'frail ... consumptive-looking' Daisy Parsons and a Mrs Farrell, with her 'loveliness of red-gold hair and ... easy-going Irish temperament'.

Sylvia recorded that at the meeting:

Our women showered protests and budgets on Runciman. Mrs Farrell declared that every week she was more in debt to the shopkeepers, Mrs Parsons that she and her children were short of food ... Mrs Drake produced the weekly budget of a mother who had eleven children to cater for ... 'Many people are considering raids on the warehouses,' she bluntly concluded, and Runciman winced perceptibly ... Mrs Payne turned on him her gaze of sorrowing humility, pleading with him that if he could see the people with their pinched faces coming to our door at Old Ford, he must feel with her the necessity of our case.

From Sylvia's account it sounds like Melvina Walker stole the show:

'It was useless to talk of a scarcity of sugar or of flour,' she insisted sharply. 'There are tons and tons of them stacked in the docks! Our men go in and see them, and they know!'

Again Runciman and his companions looked uncomfortable.

'Something must be done for us, or we shall have to take the food!' she blazed at him, striking the table.

... He answered with expressions of sympathy for our demands and our arguments; yet happily, he congratulated himself, the food had not yet reached 'panic prices'.

'Not at your salary, Mr Runciman!' Melvina Walker snapped at him, fierce as a tigress; 'but to people on 25s a week, and four or five children to bring up, they *are* panic prices!'

'It is not a question of salary,' he retorted.

She insisted: 'It *is* a question of salary!'

Whilst the East End was hit hard from the beginning, it was not until the Germans began unrestricted U-boat warfare in February 1917 that food shortages became an urgent national problem. In March of that year, 147 British ships were lost, and a full 25 per cent of all Britain-bound shipping was sunk, and tonnes of food with it. Food price controls were introduced and waste was ever more tightly regulated until at the start of 1918 the government introduced rationing.

Standing with the soldiers

> Christmas Eve night and we visit Westminster ... We hear a voice full of emotion saying: 'Will you come in and sing to us? We go to the War tomorrow.' We step inside the warm hall, where many soldiers are seated drinking tea and coffee. They are not talking, they are drinking and eating their frugal fare in almost complete silence. After we had been all entertained ... they saluted us, exchanged 'God speed,' and we passed out between soldiers drawn up at the salute. We shall never forget it! Every copper dropped into our boxes was not a mere copper, it was a wish, carried from the giver to the receiver, of comradeship, goodwill, and sister and brotherhood that will bear fruit – who knows where?
>
> Miss L. MacDonnell, 'Carolling for the E.L.F.S.',
> *The Woman's Dreadnought*, 9 January 1915

The East London Federation of the Suffragettes had always connected women's rights with the wider struggle against inequality, and had for a long time supported campaigns on issues other than votes for women. As the war went on, and more information emerged about the misery of trench warfare and new military technologies like gas, machine guns and tanks, the entire debate on suffrage shifted. It became clear that when the war was finally over, it would be impossible to deny the right to vote to the working men who had endured such horrors to defend their country. At this time, it wasn't only women who were excluded from the electoral register, but working-class men too.

In 1916, at a committee meeting, the East London Federation of the Suffragettes agreed to rename themselves the Worker's Suffrage Federation, and to expand their campaign from women's suffrage to universal adult suffrage, taking up the cause of the soldiers as well as the families they left behind. When conscription was introduced in Britain in 1916, for single men aged between 18 and 41, the Federation began immediately to campaign against it. The *Woman's Dreadnought* urged its readers not to accept conscription:

> Women, protest with all your strength and energy against Conscription ... Compulsion is dangerous to the working people and wrong in principle, and no compromise can make it either wise or just ... once the wedge is in, it will be easier to drive it further into the heart of our British liberties, than for the people to wrench it out.

Expressing anti-war sentiment at this time carried significant risks. At a Federation rally against conscription in Trafalgar Square on 8 April 1916, an unruly mob hurled red and yellow ochre at the women on the platform. Charlotte Drake's 12-year-old daughter Ruby was hit directly in the face and temporarily blinded. In December 1916 a Demonstration for Peace at the East India Dock Gates ended in confusion as the police arrested Edgar and Minnie Lansbury, along with Sylvia, Charlotte Drake and Melvina Walker, who was fined £2 for using insulting language. During another demonstration in

Victoria Park, the crowd objected to Melvina Walker's speech calling for peace. In the resulting melee, Charlotte Drake and Nellie Cressall were thrown to the ground.

In wartime, free speech is frequently curtailed, and in Britain in the First World War the instrument used was the Defence of the Realm Act, nicknamed DORA. In *The Home Front* Sylvia recalls organising a demonstration outside Holloway Prison in support of Nellie Best, who had been sentenced to six months' imprisonment under DORA: 'She had republished as a leaflet an appeal on behalf of starving and broken men discharged from the War, which had appeared in *Ainslee's Advertiser* in America … She headed the leaflet "*A Warning to those about to be Conscripted! This is how your King and country are treating the lads who voluntarily enlisted!*"'

Despite the dangers, from 1916 *The Woman's Dreadnought* became explicitly anti-militarist, openly supporting pacifists and conscientious objectors and exposing the persecution and prejudice which they routinely faced. When the *Dreadnought* published Siegfried Sassoon's now famous letter 'Finished with the war: a soldier's declaration' in August 1917, the newspaper's office was raided (not for the last time). Sylvia Pankhurst also courageously published what may be one of the earliest articles about soldiers court-martialled while suffering from 'shell shock'.

In April 1916, Sylvia went to meet a Jewish family in Whitechapel who were in the grip of intense grief after the loss of their 18-year-old son, Aby, who had joined the army soon after the war started, in September 1914. They shared his letters with her, and Sylvia printed them in the *Dreadnought*. To begin with they are not unusual – he talks about training, about how he is a little nervous about going in to the trenches, but that they are not to worry. He asks for a little money, if they can spare some.

After a short break in the letters, the family received an official notice that Aby had been injured in a mine explosion, and was recovering in hospital in France. Shortly afterwards he began to write to them again from the hospital. The letters are chatty but with occasional peculiar comments which suggest that Aby had no memory of the mine explosion – he asks his mother to tell him why he is in the hospital. After a few weeks he had apparently recovered and been returned to the front, but then the family received this alarming letter:

> Dear Mother, we were in the trenches and I was ill, so I went out and they took me to the prison, and I am in a bit of trouble now ... I will have to go in front of a Court. I will try my best to get out of it, so don't worry. I will let you know in my next letter how I get on. Give my best love to Mother, Father, and Kate. From your loving son, Aby.

Aby's mother heard nothing more from her son for almost eight fretful weeks, when the family received a chill official letter:

> Sir, I am directed to inform you that a report has been received from the War Office to the effect that No. ——, 11th Battn. Middlesex Regiment, G.S., was sentenced after trial by court martial to suffer death by being shot for desertion, and the sentence was duly executed on 20th March, 1916.

Sylvia wrote to the War Office protesting against executions for desertion and calling for compensation for Aby's parents. Her request was refused. Questions were asked in Parliament about the matter, but nothing came of them. Following the small amount of publicity around Aby's death, for fear of scandal the Army ceased to inform relatives that their sons had been executed, instead stating that they had 'died of wounds'.

Soldiers were forced to take part in firing squads, a traumatic experience in itself, as this account from a 1978 interview with dancer Victor Silvester vividly demonstrates:

> The tears were rolling down my cheeks as he went on attempting to free himself from the ropes attaching him to the chair. I aimed blindly and when the gun smoke had cleared away we were further horrified to see that, although wounded, the intended victim was still alive ... An officer in charge stepped forward to put the finishing touch with a revolver held to the poor man's temple. He had only once cried out and that was when he shouted the one word, *mother*. He could not have been much older than me. We were told later that he had in fact been suffering from shell-shock, a condition not recognised by the army at the time.

The official number of executions of British and Commonwealth soldiers such as this during the First World War is recorded as around 300, a number which was released in 1920. However, in *The Home Front*, Sylvia Pankhurst writes of an H.V. Clarke who had been employed at British headquarters in France and claimed to have viewed documents which showed that over 30,000 soldiers had been executed. In 1920 he wrote to various newspapers but none would publish his letter except *The Worker's Dreadnought*. On the day of publication Clarke's house was visited by some detectives while he was out. In a panic he destroyed his records, which he had painstakingly copied from official documents. Sylvia was contacted by the Director of Public Prosecutions and forced to print an apology and a retraction, although she remained convinced of the truth of Clarke's claims.

In autumn 1915, pioneering British nurse Edith Cavell was another victim of wartime execution – killed by a German firing squad, for helping 200 Allied soldiers escape occupied Belgium. There was an international outcry. Cavell, who trained at a nurse in the Royal London Hospital in Mile End, was celebrated for her courage and conviction, nursing and saving the lives of soldiers on both sides of the conflict. Her last words were: 'I realise that patriotism is not enough. I must have no hatred or bitterness towards anyone.'

These words struck a chord with Sylvia:

> She had grasped a tremendous truth, and had risen nobly above resentment for her execution ... In the future her story will become a great source of legend, because it typifies an important passage in social evolution. Herself of the fairest flower of patriotism, she understood that it had had its day, and must give place to its loftier successor – Internationalism.

The war raged for the first four years of the East London Federation's existence, shaping their activities, their campaigns and their aims. By the time that the war came to an end in 1918, the same year that some women were at last awarded the right to vote, it was a very different organisation. Openly socialist, pacifist, and internationalist, the Federation widened its focus from the rights and condition of women workers in East London to the rights and conditions of all workers everywhere.

Eight

WOMEN AND WORK

From the very early days of the East London Federation of the Suffragettes, its organising committee understood that to build support for votes for women they needed to connect the vote to the realities of women's daily lives. And the reality of life for most poor women in East London at this time was work. Exhausting, relentless work. Whether in a factory, a shop, a tearoom, in their own home or in a rich family's house, poor women worked just as much as their men – and often more, as they worked the 'double shift' of paid work and unpaid housework.

The East London suffragettes were contacted every week by women and girls working in appalling conditions for pitiful wages, and would help them by publicising their case in the *Dreadnought*, by helping them to organise or even lobbying their managers or local government representatives directly. The Federation also waged a long campaign for an end to sweated labour, sought equal pay for women and men, and put their philosophy into practice when they opened their own factory.

Toy Factory

In October 1914, Sylvia Pankhurst, with the financial assistance of Norah Smyth, opened the East London Toy Factory at 45 Norman Road (now Grove), in an effort to provide work for East End women who had lost their jobs through the war. The factory was run on co-operative lines and – in contrast to 'Queen Mary's Sweatshops' – the workers were paid a minimum wage of 5d an hour or £1 a week:

> It is a pleasant place, where charming toys are produced under genial conditions. No stern and rigorous discipline controls it. The rules are made by general agreement to safeguard the general standard of work, and thus benefit the entire little community. The entire value of the stock produced goes to those who work in connection with the factory.

It was an important principle of the factory that the women employed were encouraged to learn the toy-making trade. In her book *The Home Front*, Sylvia recalls how her friend Amy Browning from the Royal College of Art would come down on Saturday afternoons to teach drawing and painting to the factory workers:

> The factory was a place of happy activity, like an art school class of enthusiastic pupils. We encouraged the toy-makers to design, and if any of them produced a toy which was saleable, the factory purchased it and paid a royalty on the sales. One young mother of two toddlers, who had been employed filling sausages, developed so much skill, both as a maker and designer, that when her husband was discharged from the Army medically unfit with a small gratuity, she took him down to the South of England and started a little factory of her own there.

The East London Federation of the Suffragettes also set a precedent by opening a day nursery attached to the factory, where women could leave their children at a cost of 3d a day, including meals. This was probably the first purpose-built factory crèche in the country, and would be considered very progressive even today.

The first toys produced were simple flat wooden animals, made using wood from the Lansbury timber yard, but these became more sophisticated and a huge range of different types were introduced. A factory catalogue from 1915 lists the different types of jointed wooden toys available: pig, dachshund, hen, bird, elephant, poodle, pierrot, duck with ducklings, squirrel, fairy, dragon ... Intriguingly the list also includes toy Boy Scouts and Girl Guides, which is an indication of how quickly the scouting movement had established itself in the popular imagination – the Girl Guides Association had only been created a few years before in 1910.

Stuffed animals were also produced, and a variety of baby dolls, some with wax heads and some with moulded china heads, and in three types – a white 'British' baby, an oriental 'Japanese' baby and a black 'African' baby. These are rather remarkable for the time as they are not in any way caricatured – the African dolls look as realistic as the other types, rather than receiving the then usual 'golliwog' treatment.

An issue of *The Woman's Dreadnought* from March 1915 describes the ELFS stall at a toy fair:

> Visitors to the Toy Fair are agreed that the very best toys are to be found at the East London Federation stall, and that the stall itself is by far the most artistic in the exhibition. The interior walls of our stall are a soft grey. In the centre is a Japanese garden of pale pink almond blossom trees where the Japanese children and other toys seem to playing quite happily.

Two British babies are playing with a lamb – not one of those funny little barrel-shaped lambs with legs of stick that we have known from our childhood, but a playful babyish lamb with the big frisky clumsy legs that all real lambs have …

Another smaller British baby is clasping a white rabbit, and another sitting up amongst the squirrels looks like one of Maeterlinck's babies waiting for the ship of life to carry it into the world. Two little curly headed brown babies are holding hands and looking at each other mischievously. Three very knowing monkeys are climbing about in an orange tree.

The toys were very well received, and praised for their quality and attention to detail: even Selfridge's department store began to stock them, and they were also exhibited at the Whitechapel Art Gallery. Australian author Miles Franklin visited the factory and recalled: 'The toys are in great demand. They have orders from such firms as Marshall and Snelgrove, Liberty's and Gamage's, and many others.'

Germany was the leading manufacturer of toys at this time, and the outbreak of war created a gap in the market for British toys as imports from Germany were stopped. By chance, a German toymaker was living nearby at that time, and working at the Lansbury timber yard, a man named Niederhofer. According to Sylvia, George Lansbury was afraid to keep Niederhofer on at the yard, fearing that it would be attacked in one of the anti-German riots which erupted periodically at the start of the war. So he was employed at the toy factory at the same wage, and taught the women how to make wooden toys.

The factory was managed by a Polish woman, Mrs Regina Hercbergova, whom Sylvia appears to have intensely disliked. While Sylvia was in prison for sedition in 1921, Mrs Hercbergova took control of the factory. Although it was no longer run by the Federation it remained in business at the same location until 1934, when it moved to King's Cross, and the company was renamed Ealontoys. Like many businesses it did not survive the Second World War. One day in 1943 all but one of the staff (Andrea Silk, née Mead, who stayed to finish a piece of work) went to a nearby cafe for lunch. The cafe was destroyed by a bomb, killing most of the diners, and following this tragedy the factory was abandoned.

Munitionettes and equal pay

While factory work for less ethical employers than the suffragettes was exhausting, repetitive, poorly paid and often dangerous, it was still preferable for many young women to the more traditional route of employment open to them: domestic service. While life as a housemaid or a cook was generally deemed more 'respectable' employment than factory work by the upper classes, girls in service generally earned less than they could in the factory. Although room and board were included, many women found their freedom curtailed too far by strict rules and regulations which governed even their small amount of spare time. East Ender Maud Truphet described her experience as a housemaid:

> I used to wash their stockings and towels and had ten rooms to keep clean, for 5 shillings a week. I did all the vegetables, cleaned the kitchen pots, and when chaps came to the door, like the milkman and the greengrocer and we went to give them a cup of tea, she'd run down the stairs and listen to what we were doing, and we'd get into a row. I had one day a month off, and one evening a week – so I didn't have a lot of friends, didn't get out much …

Although it was popularly imagined that life in service helped to protect girls from the attentions of men, in fact maids were extremely vulnerable to the attentions of their male employers. Although factory work may have offered less security and respectability, many young women preferred the freedom and companionship it offered. The number of traditional domestic servants fell rapidly during the first half of the twentieth century, accelerated each time by a war. Between 1911 and 1921, the number of servants in London's commuter belt fell by half.

As the first economic shocks of the war subsided, the demand for increased production presented new opportunities for many women. Many of the factories in East London were turned over to war work, and recruited women in increasing numbers. The postal service, the railways and the buses also started recruiting women. Between 1914 and 1918, an estimated 2 million women replaced men in employment, resulting in an increase in the proportion of women in total employment from 24 per cent at the start to 37 per cent at the end of the war. It is difficult to get exact estimates because domestic workers were excluded from these figures.

Across the board, however, their pay was less than that of the men that they replaced, and most worked the infamous 'double shift' of paid work followed by unpaid childcare and housework. As the Sunderland Suffrage Society put it:

> ... the average girl and woman wage-earner has generally other responsibilities and duties. The woman 'mill-hand' often works not only all day in the mill but slaves in the evening and on Saturdays and Sundays in her home; and in all classes, even when the woman is comparatively free from such obligations, it is the general rule that a thousand and one duties fall to her which are not expected from the man wage-earner. There can be but one alternative in such cases: either the work is not

well done, or the worker breaks down, and it will have to be
recognised in the home in particular and by society in general
that girls no more than boys and women no more than men,
can burn the candle at both ends.

Sadly, this lesson is yet to be learnt in most post-industrial
societies. And although factory work was now plentiful, it was
also more dangerous, particularly for those in munitions
factories who were handling trinitrotoluene (better known as
TNT) or 'dope', a plasticised lacquer used to cover the fabric on
aircraft to make it less flammable. These women risked their
lives working with poisonous substances without adequate
protective clothing or the required safety measures.

Women who worked with TNT became known as 'canaries'
because the chemical caused their skin to turn yellow, as this
account from an anonymous munitions worker who had just
left a position filling shells with TNT shows:

> I've been pumice-stoning me 'ands for a fortnight since I left,
> to bring 'em back to the usual. I was frightened when I first
> went yeller! Yer face goes khaki ... If I'd have been there longer
> – why! I was goin' green! There was one girl there, she 'ad a
> green ribbon in 'er 'air; yer couldn't tell which was t'ribbon and
> which was 'er 'air! ... there was accidents every day we was
> there! ... An' that 'orrible fume! Yer eyes 'ud start runnin', and
> yer nose 'ud start bleedin', and yer 'adn't time even ter take out
> yer 'andkerchief ... I wouldn't 'ave stopped there if they'd give
> me sixteen pounds a week.

Some sources suggest that around 400 women died from
overexposure to TNT in Britain during the First World War.
As we have seen, many employers in the pre-war years
took a fairly relaxed attitude to the health and wellbeing of

their workers, so this certainly seems plausible. And it was a dangerous business; on Friday, 19 January 1917, just before 7 p.m., there was an enormous explosion at a munitions factory in Silvertown, West Ham: seventy-three people were killed, 400 more were injured, and the area around the factory was flattened. Newspapers the following day reported that the blast was heard and felt right across London, and the glass had been blown from the windows of the Savoy Hotel on the Strand.

In her book *The Home Front*, Sylvia Pankhurst recalls how the East London Federation of the Suffragettes received an appeal for help from some women working at an aircraft works:

> They were painting aeroplane wings with dope varnish at a wage of 15s a week, for which they had to work from 8am to 6.30pm ... There was no mess-room, and meals were often taken in the horrid atmosphere of the workshop ... It was common, they told me, for six or more of the thirty women dope painters to be lying ill on the stones outside the workshop, for half an hour, or three-quarters, before they were able to return to their toil. During a part of this period they were unconscious, and they suffered the agonising sensations of fainting, in losing and regaining consciousness. If the spell outside the workshop were not excessively prolonged, their pay was not stopped for a lack of illness. If, as often happened, they were obliged to absent themselves for a day, they were not allowed to return for a week and their pay was docked.

Through 'agitation' some small improvements in wages and working conditions were secured, and the Federation received a grateful letter from the women who pledged to support the *Dreadnought* and 'bring it to the notice of all working women'.

It was difficult for 'Munitionettes' to improve their lot as they were in the grip of the Munitions Act. Passed in 1915, the Act brought private companies supplying the Armed Forces under the tight control of the newly created Ministry of Munitions, who regulated wages, hours and employment conditions. It became a penal offence for a worker to leave their current job at one of the factories controlled by the Act without the consent of their employer, which was unsurprisingly difficult to obtain.

In May 1915 the East London Federation of the Suffragettes organised a 'Women's Exhibition' in Caxton Hall in Westminster, which included sections about the international struggle for women's suffrage in which 'charts and maps showing the progress of Woman Suffrage all over the world will be displayed, and literature will be on sale dealing with the Woman's Movement all over the world'. There was a food prices exhibit which aimed to show how far the housekeeping money would stretch before the war started, and how little it covered at the present time. Workers from the suffragette's toy factory brought some of their tasks with them, so that visitors to the exhibition could learn about the process, as well as the principles of running a business as a co-operative.

Dr Barbara Tchaykovsky was one of the first women medical doctors in Britain, and an active committee member of the East London Federation of the Suffragettes. Her contribution to the exhibition at Caxton Hall was a display about 'sweated industries', in which 'brushmakers, matchbox-makers, garment-makers and others may be seen at their accustomed work'. Controversially, the exhibition exposed the terrible pay and conditions of women working on government contracts who were being exploited in the name of 'the war effort'. The exhibition aimed to give 'unknowing and unthinking people an opportunity to judge for themselves the sweating of the women Army products, which the E.L.F.S. and others have implored the government to abolish'. As part of the exhibition, a Mrs A. from Poplar brought a pile of soldiers' trousers which she was employed to 'finish', and worked on them so that visitors could see the toil involved:

> At the Caxton Hall Mrs A has been *finishing* the soldiers' trousers at 2 ½d a pair. She has to soap the bottoms of the trousers then turn the hem and fell it. She has to put in the seat linings and what is called the 'curtain' or 'back holland', also the band of lining round the top; she has to put on twelve buttons and tack and sew part of the fly. She can finish a pair of trousers in an hour, but as the day wears on her speed diminishes ...

> She is a widow with a delicate little boy to keep. She has two sons in the Navy who are married, and one unmarried son in the Army. If what she earns were not supplemented by the allowance she gets on his account she could not live. Yet she gets up at half-past five in the morning and works until late at night, whilst her little boy helps with the housework and gets the meals ready when he comes in from school, in order that his mother need not stop her work.

> From day to day the homeworkers do not know what work will be given out to them at the factories. Sometimes they will find there is no work when they apply for it, sometimes it is better or worse paid ... Out of the 2s 6d a dozen pairs of trousers that she is paid for her work, she has to buy black and white cotton, soap and thread ... No work is given out on Saturdays, but working as hard as she can during the rest of the week she earns 7s 6d.

To put this wage in context, around this time a pound of butter cost around 1s. After lobbying for equal pay for women munitions workers, in April 1915 the government agreed to pay women the same 'piece rates' as men. That is, the same pay according to output. But no such 'special conditions' were laid down for time rates, where pay was calculated by time spent to produce the outputs. This left a big loophole for employers to continue to pay women lower wages, by switching all their work to time rates, and for the most part that is what happened.

Members of the Federation met several times with representatives from the Ministry of Munitions and the Board of Trade to make their case. Charlotte Drake outlined their argument for Christopher Addison MP on one such occasion in September 1915:

When women replace men at a lower rate of pay, as we have evidence all over the country, the employers do not stop at men of military fitness, but gradually work women right through when they are sufficiently trained. The only protection for little children is equal rate of pay for women on time rates as well as piece, as their fathers are thrown out of work.

The minimum wage must be a living one of 7d an hour or 28s a week of 48 hours … The Munitions Act, instead of aiming at better production, aims at controlling workers more, instead of taking into consideration conditions under which the workers work, and trade union rates of pay. Its object should be the output in the interest of all. At the present it is simply a slave driver for the workers, causing great bitterness and having a prejudicial effect on everything.

The committees set up to deal with the question of women's labour as replacing the labour of men are a scandal, as only two women are on them. This is owing to women's voteless condition, but should be at once remedied by placing women only and entirely on committees to manage the conditions, wages and hours of women and girls.

Equal pay for women was sadly still a long way off, and after the war many employers and trade unions acted not only to reduce women's pay but to push women out of the workforce altogether. We have had equal pay legislation in Britain since the Equal Pay Act of 1970, but there is still a stubborn gap between the average wages of women and men, and although we now have a national minimum wage, many employers fail to pay a true living wage.

'Girls, all join the union'

One legacy of the war was a big increase in women's trade-union membership. Previously, women were much less likely to be unionised than their male counterparts. This was partly because they tended to do part-time work, work in smaller firms, or work at home, and partly because existing unions were often hostile to women in the workforce. During the war the unions couldn't hide from 'the woman question' any longer. In 1914 just 357,000 women were in a trade union, but by 1918 that figure had risen to over a million, an increase of 160 per cent.

Women's role in trade union history is still being uncovered, but it's plain to see in the pages of *The Woman's Dreadnought*, which regularly reported on the activities of organised women workers:

In our last issue but one, we reported that the women of Scott's Tin Box Factory, Deptford, had won their strike. On May 27th, 300 women at Lloyds Tin Box Factory, nearby, also struck for an increase in wages and the abolition of fines. At present the women time workers receive 8s a week and the piece workers 5s, 6s and 7s a week. The fines are excessive, and in one week recently two women were each fined 4s 6d!

The workers at Pink's Jam Factory in Bermondsey, after a plucky stand, have won but very little, viz.: that the Wages Board rates are to be paid a month before they actually come into operation, and that the degrading habit of searching, to which no woman ought to be called upon to submit, shall be performed in the firm's time and not after working hours.

The women workers at Messrs G.W. Rosenthal, makers of 'Rego' clothing, Bethnal Green Road, are on strike. The piece-work rates paid are said to be 50 per cent lower than those paid elsewhere. The women have to stitch 168 buttonholes on vests for 4d. There are deductions for cotton etc.

By organising and campaigning together for better conditions, women gained not only material improvements but an opportunity to express their creativity, subversion and sense of humour and challenge the confines of a rigid work hierarchy in which 'the bosses' wielded a huge amount of power. A few months before the war, on 19 March 1914, the *Daily Mail* published a picture of young women dancing in the street, under the headline 'Tango Dancing Girl Strikers'.

Three hundred women workers of Messrs. C and E Morton, provision merchants, West Ferry Road, Millwall, had come out on strike to protest against a management ploy to undercut wages by recruiting younger workers. Soon all the employees, 1,000 women and girls and 600 men, were on strike.

The *Daily Herald* reported on 25 March that the picket line outside the factory was holding and that public feeling was entirely in support of the strikers. Meetings were held regularly in the Millwall Cinema and the strikers were addressed by Lena Ashwell, a West End stage actress and producer. Mary MacArthur, secretary of the National Federation of Women Workers, and Susan Lawrence, London County Council member for Poplar, helped to organise the women strikers. The strikers held a huge rally, marching procession in around Millwall and singing 'strike songs', one to the tune of 'Every nice girl loves a sailor' with following words:

> Messrs. Morton, down at Poplar,
> Don't you think it a disgrace
> To employ little children
> Women workers to displace;
> Many years we've faithful served you,
> And your profits have been great,
> So the reason is quite clear
> Why we're standing idle here
> At your gate, at your gate.
>
> For we know that when the children
> Do our work for half our pay
> You won't hesitate a moment
> But will send us all away;
> And your boxes will be soldered
> At the nearest infant schools,
> So we've all gone out on strike,
> For the prospect we don't like,
> We're not fools, we're not fools.
>
> Now then, girls, all join the Union,
> Whatever you may be,
> In pickles, jam or chocolate,

Or packing pounds of tea;
For we all want better wages,
And this is what we say:
We're out to right the wrong,
And now we shan't be long,
Hip Hurrah! Hip Hurrah!

The strike lasted twelve days before the management, overwhelmed by the public support the strikers received, and embarrassed by the media coverage showing the girls singing and dancing in the streets, gave in to the strikers' demands.

As well as economic opportunities the war brought with it irrevocable social changes, including unprecedented freedoms for working women, for whom the liberated lifestyle of the 1890s' New Woman was out of reach. Women began to wear trousers, to smoke in public, and roam unaccompanied by men – even have their dinner in restaurants with a female friend or even alone. As the war went on, in spite of their poverty and hardship, many working women developed a greater confidence in themselves and determination to secure a better life. This report from a factory supervisor in the *New Statesman* hints at the dramatic changes which were to come in post-war Britain, as young women rebelled in ever greater numbers against the expectations of their class and their gender which had been forged in the Victorian era:

... they appear more alert, more critical of the conditions under which they work, more ready to take a stand against injustice than their pre-war selves of the prototypes. They have a keener appetite for experience and pleasure and a tendency quite new to their class to protest against wrongs even before they become 'intolerable'.

Nine

FOOD AND FAMILY

One of the great strengths of the East London Federation of the Suffragettes, and one of the things that made them unique, was the way they intertwined their principled call for women's suffrage with practical community action to improve the conditions in which their members lived. They launched a number of successful initiatives which helped to alleviate the suffering of some of the most vulnerable in society, from young children to the very elderly. Somehow they found time alongside this work to put on summer festivals and Christmas parties for local children, a testament to the high value they placed on the community and their place in it.

Housing

Many East End dwellings at this time were little changed from the Victorian slums vividly portrayed in the works of Dickens. The tenements were falling apart, full of vermin and densely overcrowded, often with a family of six living in a single room.

Most of the Federation's committee members had been born and lived in East London, so the terrible conditions were very familiar. But even incomers like Sylvia, Zelie Emerson and Norah Smyth lived in Bow for many years, and had direct experience of some of the problems. In her book *The Suffragette Movement*, Sylvia remembers the room in which she stayed when recovering from her hunger strikes and the trauma of force-feeding. The room was one of just two in which her friend Mrs Jessie Payne lived with her husband ('the kindest of kind people') at 28 Ford Road, Bow:

> Mrs Payne told me that as a young bride she hung her bed with pink curtains, but plunged those curtains into a bucket of water the night of her marriage on account of the bugs she was horrified to find crawling over them. When I lit my candle on sleepless nights, I would see a dozen or more of them on the wall, though disinfectants were always burnt in the room during my absence.

Like many East End families the Paynes lived and worked in their two rooms, making shoes and boots. The range of different types of work that Sylvia could observe just from one window gives a powerful sense of how much activity and human life was packed into the little streets of Bow:

> The next yard was a fish curers'. An old lady with a chenille net on her grey hair would be passing in and out of the smoke-house, preparing the sawdust fires. A man with his shirt sleeves rolled up would be splitting herrings; and another hooking them on to rods balanced on boards and packing cases, till the yard was filled and gleamed with them like a coat of mail. Close by, tall sunflowers were growing, and garments of many colours were hung out to dry. Next door to us they bred pigeons and

cocks and hens, which cooed and crowed and clucked in the early hours. Two doors away a woman supported a paralysed husband and number of young children by making shirts at 8d a dozen.

It is worth taking a moment to note the contrast between this account and the 'slum literature' quoted at the beginning of this book. Although Sylvia was acutely aware of the horrors of abject poverty, she writes about the East End and its inhabitants with respect and compassion, referring continually to the dignity, industry, friendship and generosity that she found there. In her accounts, East Enders are individuals with hopes and cares, not an animal mass seething at the edge of the city.

With so many people in East London being charged high rents for terrible housing, the East London Federation of the Suffragettes hit upon a way to put pressure on landlords to improve housing *and* keep up the pressure on government to give women the right to vote: a 'No Vote, No Rent' strike. This article from *The Woman's Dreadnought* calls on the inhabitants of a particularly bad slum – the area around Brady Street in Bethnal Green – to join the strike:

It is many years since 60 out of every 100 of the houses in the Brady Street area of Bethnal Green were condemned as unfit for human habitation … Nothing was done and these miserable dwellings are still densely overcrowded with human beings. The number of persons to an acre in the Brady Street area is 408, though 50 persons an acre is considered to be the healthy standard.

There is a death rate in this district of 24 per 1,000 as compared with the death rate of 17 per 1,000 for the remainder of the

Borough, and 13 per 1,000 for the whole of London. The houses are in the last stages of disrepair, yet such high rents as 5s 6d and 6s 6d a week are charged for two miserable rooms. In these rooms large families are herded together. One visitor to Lisbon Street recently found two families residing side by side, each occupying two rooms and each consisting of a mother, father and eight children. Another visitor to Lisbon Street was told by a nursing mother that the newly patched ceiling had fallen down on her the night her baby was born ...

The dwellers in the Brady Street area should be amongst the first to join the 'No Vote No Rent' Strike ... When men were fighting for the franchise they refused to pay their taxes until they obtained the power to vote for them. The 'No Vote No Rent' Strike is a stronger weapon, and the state of affairs in the Brady Street area shows that the strikers need have no pity for the landlords.

Then as now women were largely held responsible for the health and wellbeing of their children, for the cleanliness and comfort of their home and the provision of nutritious meals for their family. When children were not well, when the house was not clean, and when food was not available, women were frequently blamed for their poor housekeeping, particularly if they were working outside the home. The suffragettes made the case that many of the factors which influenced the health and happiness of their family were in fact well beyond women's control, including poor housing. Mothers struggled in the face of unsanitary plumbing, buildings falling to pieces, widespread vermin and disease. Among those who could change the situation were national and local government representatives, and by extension those who voted for them: 'If we hold women responsible for the results, must we not, in simple justice, let them have something to say as to what these conditions shall be? ... Let them vote.'

Ultimately the 'No Vote No Rent' campaign was curtailed by the outbreak of war, when the Federation's resources were needed for other initiatives. However, poor housing continued to be an area of concern, and the suffragettes supported campaigns by local residents, including the 516 families housed in the Grosvenor Buildings, on the corner of Robinhood Lane and Manisty Street in Poplar, who faced a sudden rent hike in the winter of 1915:

> All the tenants object to this increase and have told us that they intend to refuse to pay it ... The ELFS notified Mr Yeo, the local MP, and our Poplar Branch has taken the matter up, and arranged meetings ... A petition signed by the tenants, together with the following resolution have been sent to Government representatives:

> 'That this meeting of soldiers' wives and other working women and housewives, protests against the raising of the rents of working class dwellings, which in reality is a device to force the working classes to pay the extra income tax and other expenses of landlords arising out of the War; and recognising that the working classes already pay a heavier share of war taxes as consumers of tea, sugar, and other commodities than their incomes warrant, this meeting calls upon the Government to take immediate action to prevent the raising of rents during the War.'

Although there were some improvements to housing in East London after the First World War, it was not until after the devastation of the Blitz in the Second World War that there was widespread change. The post-war tower blocks and estates familiar to all East Londoners brought their own problems, but many former slum residents were delighted with their new flats – no more collapsing ceilings and bedbugs, and running water and indoor toilets were a welcome novelty.

The Mother's Arms

Within weeks of the start of the First World War in August 1914, the impact was felt in the East End. Numerous families were suddenly deprived of all income as reservists were called up to join the war and factories closed. Bureaucratic chaos meant that many soldiers' wives didn't receive their separation allowance for months, in the meantime they were forced to pawn all their belongings and let themselves and their children go hungry.

The East London Federation of the Suffragettes began distributing milk to feed starving infants from their Women's Hall at 400 Old Ford Road. Over the next few weeks, other war relief offices were opened, first at 319 East India Dock Road, and Crowder Hall, Bow Road, and then at Poplar Women's Hall at 20 Railway Street and 53 St Leonard's Street, Bromley. Later, under the direction of Daisy Parsons, a centre was opened in Canning Town, first at Butcher's Road, and later at 55 Fife Road.

Soon all these centres were providing free milk to mothers with babies, together with Virol, eggs and barley, as well as free leaflets and feeding charts about infant health. Donations poured in, including 3s from 'Meg Thompson, aged 5 … for the "poor little babies in East London"'. Good work, Meg! Interestingly, the *Dreadnought* gives thanks for corporate sponsorship in the form of milk and baby food from two familiar (and now rather infamous) companies: Nestlé and Glaxo, which went on to become GlaxoSmithKline.

Whilst attendance at these milk depots grew, and babies started to thrive on the nourishment provided, it was felt that more could be done for the rest of the family. The Federation opened their toy factory on 45 Norman Grove to provide employment, and included a crèche where working mothers could leave their children during the day. The nursery opened on 17 October 1914:

> It is delightfully fresh and bright. There are gay-coloured pictures on the white walls from which the marks made by little fingers can be washed off every day. There is a wonderful doll's house sent by Lady Sybil Smith's children who have been adding treasures to it for ten years. There is a shop, a doll's perambulator and there are numbers of dolls, teddy bears, brick and tile boxes, and all sorts of other toys. The charge for a child's day in the nursery from 8am to 7pm, including meals, is 3d.

Sybil Smith was one of the Federation's upper-class supporters. Four days a week she left 'the social round of Mayfair' to manage the nursery in Bow. As well as the magnificent dolls' house she brought 'a host of more useful trophies which could be abstracted unnoticed from her charming home at Rolls Park, Chigwell', as well as one of her children's former nurses. She also hosted meetings at her home to collect funds for the ELFS, at which Sylvia spoke and Sybil sang.

The nursery was very popular – so popular, in fact, that a second, larger nursery was opened nearby the following year. On the corner of Old Ford Road and St Stephen's Road was a disused public house, which at one time was called the Gunmakers' Arms, as it lay opposite a weapons factory. Sylvia and her colleagues set to work refurbishing the place, and in April 1915, the Mother's Arms opened as a mother and baby clinic, free milk depot and day nursery. The letters ELFS were painted in gold on the outside, surrounded by red caps of liberty. Bessie Lansbury, wife of former local MP George Lansbury, took on the role of director of the Mother's Arms.

In July 1915 'A. Visitor' recorded their impressions of the nursery in *The Woman's Dreadnought*:

> A bright, fresh coloured young nurse brought me to more cheerful surroundings. The children who are brought in the morning to stay have a grand, spacious, light and airy nursery, everything scrupulously clean. Dainty little cots where the babies were sleeping, others were lying on stretchers, all apparently tired after their morning airing in the park.

A regular clinic was staffed by two doctors, Alice Johnson and Barbara Tchaykovsky, a London County Council school doctor, with the support of Nurse Maud Hebbes, who was later to become the first nurse at Marie Stopes' Birth Control Clinic. The same anonymous visitor comments on the sad condition of many of the infants brought in to the clinic:

> I had never seen an East End baby, by that I mean the child of an overworked, ill-fed woman. I saw a few to-day and I fear I shall never forget it! All the agony and want of the parents seemed imprinted on the child's countenance, and its limbs were just like blades of grass, so thin and scraggy – all the care possible would hardly keep that infant alive, and yet were it not for the care of the E.L.F.S. I do not suppose anyone would trouble much what became of it!

There is one photo in particular among the many taken by Norah Smyth which bears witness to this account and others like it: a tiny child held in the lap of Nurse Hebbes. The child is gaunt, arms and legs like sticks and the outline of its skull clearly visible in its face beneath a thatch of fair hair. It is a shocking image, and acts effectively to puncture any romantic visions of the jolly poverty of the old East End.

Respect and admiration for the work of the doctors and nurses at the Mother's Arms grew and they were soon receiving referrals from other local doctors:

> As a last resort, our doctor ordered into the day nursery a year old baby, reduced almost to a skeleton, whom she thought would certainly die. This child has been treated with sea-water injections, and carefully nursed and nourished, and after a week's stay, has recovered so wonderfully that the doctor expects its condition to be normal at the end of another week.

Stories such as this bring home the importance of the East London Federation of the Suffragettes' work in Bow and the surrounding area at this desperate time. They not only changed lives, but saved them.Because the importance and positive impact of their work was so immediately apparent, the Mother's Arms attracted a good deal of publicity and support, receiving grants from the Corporation of London and the Ministry of Health and the Ministry of Education. As ever, though, it was the support of the community in Bow which helped to keep the project alive, as Australian writer Miles Franklin observed when she visited the Mother's Arms during her time in England:

> The people round about are very generous, and voluntarily the workers in the munitions and clothing factories across the way have asked for collection boxes through which about £3 per week comes in, one of the workers giving up her time to do the work of collection.

It is remarkable to think that just two years previously the suffragettes were considered to be dangerous radicals, subject to state repression and police surveillance. On 5 October 1914 a journalist in the *Evening Times* observed that:

> Once again the suffragettes are showing that whatever may be their faults in other directions they are organisers of rare genius. These powers of organisation, which in the past have been chiefly engaged in terrorising the nation, are now being devoted to a very splendid and patriotic aim. Down in East London, where the slightest cog in the economic machine means acute misery ... the whole energies of the suffragettes' splendid organisation are being bent towards relieving the distress.

The Mother's Arms was a success. In 1916 writer Israel Zangwill gave a speech at the opening of a second Women's Exhibition at Caxton Hall, and said:

> ... the hope of the world lies in changing the Gunmaker's Arms into the Mother's Arms. I trust that our Sylvia's action will be symbolic of the whole future course of history; for we will not pretend here that we are saving these babies merely that they may grow up to be food for cannon!

That year Sylvia grew concerned about the destructive tendencies of the little children that came to them. Sybil Smith donated a beautiful wooden rocking horse for the nursery:

> ... within a month, it was no more. Every hair of the tail and mane had gone; the eyes were gouged out, every joint in the wood severed; the remnants had been torn from their stand. To me it was amazing that young children under five years of age

could have done it. To the busy staff at the nursery it was all a matter of course ...

One day Sylvia read in the newspaper that suffragette Muriel Matters had returned from a year in Barcelona studying with Maria Montessori. Sylvia immediately contacted her and Muriel agreed to begin the Montessori Method with the older children at the Mother's Arms.

Muriel Matters was an Australian journalist, actress and educator who had been an active member of the Women's Freedom League. One of her most remarkable exploits was a trip in a rickety airship with 'VOTES FOR WOMEN' painted on the side in huge letters, from which she scattered leaflets about the cause over the streets of London. Speaking about the incident in a BBC radio interview in later life she commented thoughtfully: 'Daring? I suppose it was daring ...'

Equally daring, although in a different way, was Maria Montessori herself. Montessori flouted social convention to study medicine and education. She was the first female doctor in Italy, and built on her study of child development to pioneer a controversial new educational approach which aimed to build children's independence rather than obedience. She believed that a learning environment in which children were encouraged to explore ideas independently at their own pace and treated as autonomous individuals would increase their motivation to learn and help them to fulfil their potential. The 'Montessori Method' emphasised the development of initiative and natural abilities, in particular through practical play, and it is still used throughout the world today.

A few weeks after their telephone conversation, Muriel Matters arrived in Bow and the first Montessori nursery school in Britain was opened at the Mother's Arms. Muriel ordered that no physical discipline was to be used on the children.

Instead, when they were disorderly they were sent from the classroom to the nursery to spend an hour or two with the babies as they were evidently 'not yet old enough' to take part. At times there were just one or two children left in the classroom, but within a few days all the children had been won over. Soon they were serving each other tea from dainty china cups, where before the cups would quickly have been smashed to smithereens.

The Mother's Arms was one of the East London Federation of the Suffragettes' most successful projects, and finally closed its doors two years after the end of the war, in 1921.

Cost price restaurants

Another East London Federation of the Suffragettes initiative launched to fight the hunger of the war's early years was a series of 'cost price' restaurants, which served nutritious hot food for very low prices. 'Cost price' was intended as a 'slogan against profiteering', and the Federation aimed to serve 'two-penny, two-course meals to adults, penny meals to children, at midday; and each evening a pint of hot soup and a chunk of bread for a penny; to be consumed on the premises or taken home'.

Aware of the intense stigma attached to charity among the proud East End people, the suffragettes came up with an ingenious method to help those who could not even afford the few pence for a bowl of soup:

> Tickets for the meal, or books of tickets to last the week, would be purchased at the door. To people wholly without means we should supply free tickets, and no one at the tables would be aware whether the tickets of the people beside them had been purchased or given free.

Gifts of crockery, utensils, chickens, vegetables, homemade pickles and jam poured in from local supporters, and some anonymous benefactors:

> For many months twelve loaves of bread reached us daily; from whom we never knew. When they ceased there was a sense of loss – as though a friend had died – killed in the War, perhaps; we never knew. For a year or more a man called occasionally in the evening, laid down a bundle of money with a muffled word and hurried away. We never knew his name or what became of him.

The first restaurant was opened at 400 Old Ford Road, with others following at the other women's centres at 20 Railway Street in Poplar and 53 Leonard Street in Bromley. All three became very popular, and the provision of meals for over 100 people each mealtime with very scant facilities was no mean feat. As Miles Franklin observed admiringly: 'Dear me, what courage, industry and sheer grit it takes to keep clean these ramshackle, mouldy places with the tin-pot means of accomplishment at hand.'

Some objected to the restaurants, believing that they would compete with existing restaurants and coffee shops and damage their business. The Federation addressed this concern in *The Woman's Dreadnought*:

> Women and children come to the 'Cost Price' restaurants, not because they can get their meals more cheaply than at any other restaurant, but because they can get them more cheaply than in their own homes, now that prices have gone up so high: and because they are spared the labour of cooking meals now that they have been obliged to do more paid work, either in the factory or in the home.

Run by health-food enthusiasts Mrs Ennis Richmond and her sister Morgan Brown, the restaurants provided scrupulously healthy meals, which were reportedly not always to the taste of the clientele. Potatoes were added to stews skins on, for example. Sadly no recipes from the restaurant menus were printed in *The Woman's Dreadnought*, so we don't know exactly what dishes were served. However, in 1914 the newspaper did print an article called 'What to Eat in Wartime' by a 'Nurse Startup' which advocated vegetarianism and included a number of recipes which may give us a flavour:

Put half lb of butter beans in a basin over night, and cover with cold water. Next morning directly after breakfast, turn them straight into a casserole or covered jar, water as well as beans. Add a piece of nutter [nut oil butter] the size of two walnuts, cover tight, with the lid, and put in a moderate oven. About ten minutes before serving add some chopped parsley. Some green vegetables should be served with this. When in season spinach is very good …

If there are some beans left over they may be mashed up with a tomato, a grated raw onion, a little sage or thyme and enough breadcrumbs to make it stiff enough to roll into balls or sausages. Beat up one egg, mix half with the mixture, dip each ball or sausage into the other half, and roll in brown bread crumbs and fry in nutter. This with fried potatoes will make a tasty dinner for the next day.

Another easy dish which makes a nourishing meal, is – Put two tomatoes in boiling water for a minute, then skin and put them into a covered saucepan or casserole. Cook about five minutes. Beat up two eggs, pour over the tomatoes, add two teaspoonsful of Grape Nuts and a little celery salt, and scramble together. Serve on four slices of thick brown bread, toasted and buttered hot …

Several more column inches are devoted to the joys of nutter and strict instructions not to add salt and pepper.

War babies

One of the concerns at the outbreak of the war was the impact on Britain's social fabric and moral fibre of the home front, in particular on the morals of girls and young women and irresponsible young soldiers out for a good time. The indicator of moral decline was held to be the number of children born to unmarried mothers, the dreaded 'war babies'.

At this time there was no child-maintenance legislation, and unmarried mothers had no entitlement to an allowance from the War Office if the father was a soldier, even if the father did want to support the child. In the early years of the war some advocated a relaxation of the antiquated laws regarding the rights of illegitimate children and argued that the state should support the inevitable tide of war babies as part of their patriotic duty. But the stigma of unmarried motherhood was powerful, and behind the handwringing there lay many tragic stories in which women and girls fell foul of the punishing sexual double standard, which meant that once a woman was held to be 'fallen' she was essentially an outcast. One such story is found in a sad letter to the *Daily Herald* which was reprinted in *The Woman's Dreadnought* in May 1915:

> My little sister Kitty, who is not quite 15, having been got into trouble by a soldier who was billeted at her mistress's house at Saint Albans, has been turned out of her place. She went home to

father and stepmother, hoping they would help her in her trouble, but they was so mad at the disgrace they would not let her inside the door. So she came tramping here (Woolwich) to find me, where I was in service, and the result was that my mistress told us we could both go, though I had always had a good character.

I soon found work for myself in a factory and room to sleep in, but the landlady will not have Kitty in the house, as she does not want no babies born there. So I have had to take the poor little soul to a women's lodging house at 6d a night. And she has got to wander about all day or sit down to rest on the common, where men will not leave her alone, as they cannot stop there in the daytime. I don't want her to have to go to the workhouse, as we was both brought up decent when mother was alive ...

If any of your readers could have seen her as I last saw her at home, a pretty little laughing girl with short frocks and curls hanging down her back, and to see her as she is now, ill and wretched and all the laugh gone out of her, eight months gone with the child, and dragging round in an old long skirt of mine to hide her shame the best we can, I am sure they would pity her.

It is noted that arrangements were being made to find a better home and some employment for the girl, but there were undoubtedly many others who did not find the same support. Although the Federation didn't launch any projects specifically about unmarried mothers, Sylvia records examples of her involvement in some individual cases. One issue of *The Woman's Dreadnought* features a letter 'From a War Father' who is umming and ahhing about whether to provide a 'small allowance' for a lower-class girl who he has made pregnant. Does his discovery that she already has another child relieve him of any moral obligation? The editor responds, angrily:

> You say 'she is not the class of girl' for you … But in what are you better than she? She has entered into the sexual relationship out of wedlock: so have you. In *that* you are both equal … You will say, perhaps, that nature and the law have forced her to accept a greater responsibility than that which you will take. Yes, it is true, nature has placed the heavier share of the burden on the woman, whether the child be born according to our little lawyer's rules or not. Man-made society has added to the burden. But women are coming slowly into their own. Slowly the rights of the child begin to be understood.

Many would find Sylvia Pankhurst's views on sex, motherhood and marriage radical even today, as she advocated love and sexual union without marriage, but with free state support available for all mothers and their children. In 1930 she published a pamphlet called *Save Our Mothers* which called for a national non-contributory maternity benefit, allowances for children, free pre- and post-natal healthcare for mothers and infants and the raising of the school age to 16. The pamphlet was well received, and Ramsay MacDonald, leader of the Labour Party and Prime Minister of the next Labour government, adopted many of her proposals.

Old and young

In August 1916 Sylvia and Miriam Price led a delegation of twenty old-age pensioners to the House of Commons to lobby for an increase on the 5s a week which they currently received. None had been inside Parliament before and many had never even visited the centre of London. They were delighted to be invited to tea on the Terrace by Liberal MP James Hogge, as Sylvia remembered:

They admired the pigeons, the water, the architecture, the little tables with snow-white cloths, the waiters resplendent; their eyes sparkled at sight of butter, real butter, plastered thick on dainty thin slices of bread, and cubes of sparkling white sugar supplied without stint.

The pensioners argued with officials that they could not subsist on the existing allowance, and gave examples of their careful budgets, pointing out that 152 old-age pensioners had been forced to enter the workhouse in Edinburgh in the previous year because they could not survive on the meagre pension. That afternoon Prime Minister Asquith announced a small concession: grants up to 2s 6d a week would be made available to old-age pensioners in cases of severe hardship.

That same summer of 1916 saw one of the finest of the events which the East London Federation of the Suffragettes laid on for hundreds of local children: a Children's Festival in Victoria Park. From their very early days the Federation understood the importance of building support for the suffrage cause among the whole community, but they also had a genuine desire to bring some 'brightness and joy' to the lives of the children in their neighbourhood.

Previous events had included a New Year's party held at Bow Baths Hall which featured music, games, and an elaborate pageant in which local children dressed as lilies (Mary and Nellie Cohen), 'the Spirit of Liberty' (Lily Gatward) or 'the Spirit of Peace' (Joan Beauchamp, who appropriately enough became editor of pacifist publication the *Conscientious Objectors' Tribunal* many years later, and even served a prison term for it). George Lansbury and a Mr Hobday put on a puppet show, and Father Christmas (the long-suffering Norah Smyth) even made a belated appearance, presenting all 900 excited children in attendance with a small gift, 'with untiring good humour'.

One sad story is attached to this happy event, however. One of the photographs of the pageant shows a 16-year-old girl called Rose Pengelly dressed as 'The Spirit of the Woods' and playing the Pipes of Pan. Although we do not know much about Rose, what we do know shows she was a remarkable girl – she was beautiful, with green eyes and red hair, and lived with her very poor family on Ranwell Street in Bow. She joined the 'Junior Suffragette Club' created by the Federation in 1914, and in her early teens worked at the Backs Asbestos Pipe Factory on Old Ford Road. In an issue of *The Woman's Dreadnought* she described how she had to pack the heavy 'saggers of ware', and carry them to the furnace. She also ran errands for the housekeeper, peeled potatoes and even washed 'the governor's' shirts and sheets.

Aged 14, Rose led her colleagues out on strike, marching them down the road to the Women's Hall. She lost her job because of her union activism, and was thereafter nicknamed 'Sylvia' by her friends and former colleagues. Two years later, at the time of the pageant, she had found another position, operating a machine in a different factory. Just two days after she appeared in the New Year's pageant, she caught her hand in the machine she was working on. Her new employer refused to offer her any assistance, so 16-year-old Rose, bleeding heavily, walked to Bow station and took the train to the London Hospital at Mile End, where the thumb and two fingers of her right hand were amputated. There is no record of what happened to Rose after the accident, but her story serves to underline the callous indifference of many employers to their workers, many of whom were no more than children.

Incidents like this were sadly common among the families of the East End at this time, which was one of the reasons that the celebrations for children were so important. Many children took on work of various kinds while they were still at school, and most left school before they were 16. With barely enough money to keep a roof over their heads and put food on the table, there was little spare for toys and treats for younger children, and the closest thing that many families had to a holiday was hop-picking in Kent in the summer months. The suffragettes' Children's Festival in June 1916 was a day-long party held in Victoria Park, which included refreshments, games, music and various races and athletic competitions for the boys and girls. The show-stopping feature was a pageant, organised by Sylvia Pankhurst's cousin Sylvia Bailey:

> Sixty little girl dancers, wearing white dresses and garlanded with flowers, marched in procession by a roundabout route to the Park, followed by all the boys and girls of the neighbourhood, whilst the mothers came running out to see the show. The dancing took place in the centre of the ring of trees on the mound beyond the racing track. The audience formed a circle round. The children danced very charmingly and gaily without a trace of shyness or affectation, and with a light suppleness which is characteristic of little Londoners. One of the audience was heard to say that the scene was idyllic, and calculated to make the children wish for a more beautiful life than that of the crowded slums.

Ten

LATER YEARS

Three events in the last years of the 1910s effectively brought the East London Federation of the Suffragettes to an end. In January 1918, the Representation of People Act granted the vote to women over the age of 30, subject to a small property qualification. In November 1918, the war against which they had struggled and which had shaped so much of their work, finally came to an end. But more significant than both of these, in October 1917 the Bolsheviks seized power in Russia.

Votes for (some) women

Rae Strachey of the National Union of Women's Suffrage Societies was in the Ladies' Gallery of the House of Commons on the day of the decisive vote on women's suffrage on 19 June 1917:

> For all their certainty, the women … were desperately excited. Often, as some of them had sat there before, to hear their cause mocked at, or obstructed, or outvoted in the chamber below,

the scene was painfully impressive. Through the bars of the absurd little cage in which they were penned, they saw chiefly the tops of the heads of the legislators, but the atmosphere of excitement which pervaded the House was noticeable even so ... The tide had really turned, and when the time for the division came there were found to be but 55 opponents in the whole House, while 385, seven times their number, went into the other Lobby. This vote was larger than even the most optimistic had expected. It was victory without reserve.

Despite this excitement, the Act was met with muted celebration. 'Gone was the mirage of a society regenerated by enfranchised womanhood as by a magic wand,' Sylvia Pankhurst wrote. 'Men and women had been drawn closer together by the suffering and sacrifice of the War.'

Although women were now able to stand for election as Members of Parliament (and local Poplar guardian Susan Lawrence was one of the first to successfully do so) Sylvia was cynical about the extent of change which could be achieved through the parliamentary route, believing that the women who entered Parliament 'will go in and play the sad old party game that achieves so little' whereas those who remain outside, 'the more active and independent women', would remain 'a discontented crowd of rebels'.

In 1916 the East London Federation of the Suffragettes had changed its name to the Worker's Suffrage Federation, and embraced the cause of the working men at the front and conscientious objectors at home, and added the call for working men's suffrage to their call for women's suffrage. In 1917 *The Woman's Dreadnought* became *The Worker's Dreadnought*, and although it maintained its interest in women's rights, the content became more focused on the international socialist movement. It also branched out beyond East London, with branches in Hoxton, Islington, Holloway and Holborn. By 1917 there were Worker's Suffrage Federation branches in many different areas of England, Wales and Scotland.

The extension of the franchise in 1918 necessitated another name change, and the Worker's Suffrage Federation became the Worker's Socialist Federation in May 1918. In fact the Federation had gradually changed its emphasis over the previous year, becoming a feminist, socialist organisation rather than a socialist, feminist organisation. For example, the report from the Federation's annual conference in June 1917 listed working towards abolishing capitalism as one of its chief task, and 'the establishment of a socialist commonwealth in which the means of production and distribution shall be deployed in the interests of the people'.

The February and October revolutions in Russia had a profound effect on the British left wing, including the Worker's Suffrage Federation, which was one of the first groups to publicly support the Bolsheviks. The *Dreadnought* carried pro-revolutionary articles and reports from Russia, as well as increasing numbers of articles about Marxist theory. In July 1918, Sylvia established the People's Russian Information Bureau, which included individuals from the Independent Labour Party, the British Socialist Party and others. Its goal was to provide reliable information about the events taking place in Russia.

One of the Workers' Socialist Federation's members at this time was Harry Pollitt, who later became General Secretary of the Communist Party. In 1919 Pollitt was living in a basement bedroom in Poplar and working as a ship repairer. He spoke on behalf of the Federation and contributed articles to the *Dreadnought*. He also worked on the 'Hands Off Russia' campaign which aimed to build solidarity between British workers and the workers in Russia, and encouraged dockers to refuse to load boxes of munitions intended to suppress the revolution. Pollitt was good friends with Melvina Walker, and recalled how 'Mrs Walker of Poplar toiled like a Trojan, on a shopping morning you could rely on seeing her in Crisp Street, talking to groups of women about Russia and how we must help, asking them to tell their husbands to keep their eyes skinned to see that no munitions went to those trying to crush the revolution.'

While socialism was an alarming prospect for many, the word did not have all the same negative associations that it does today. Although the Federation lost a great deal of supporters throughout these changes, it gained others and the *Dreadnought* circulation figures stayed strong. In fact, the newly formed Communist Party of Great Britain (whose founders included early East London suffragette Adelaide Knight, her husband Donald and her friend Dora Montefiore) attempted to make the *Dreadnought* the official party newspaper in 1921, but Sylvia refused. She was expelled from the party.

The Federation and *The Worker's Dreadnought* continued until 1924 when both were finally closed down; Sylvia moved from Bow to Woodford in Essex, and Norah Smyth settled in Italy. Though never a 'star' of the suffragette movement, Smyth played countless crucial roles, from drilling the People's Army to dressing up as Father Christmas. Miles Franklin described her as 'equally capable' as Sylvia, and admired the way she could 'turn her hand from fitting out a baby to driving a motor car, as the necessity arises'. And of course it is Norah's remarkable photographs that bring the Federation's work alive today.

Sylvia

Although Sylvia ultimately grew disillusioned with communism she never lost her radical spirit or her determination to challenge injustice. In Woodford she founded an orphanage and erected an anti-war memorial. Annie Barnes, who stayed friends with Sylvia, recalls visiting her at this time:

> We used to take groceries because we knew there'd not be much in the house to eat. When we arrived she was usually busy. We'd go into the kitchen and make a meal for everyone; the house was always full of people. One time we couldn't find any saucepans. The girl who'd been doing the cooking had gone off and taken the lot. Sylvia didn't seem bothered – she just said, 'I expect she needs them more than I do.'

Sylvia was living with her partner, Italian anarchist Silvio Corio, and their home, the Red Cottage, became a haven for political refugees, in particular those who had been persecuted for helping Jews to flee fascism. At the age of 45 she gave birth to her only child, a son they named Richard. This was scandalous not just because of Sylvia's age, but because she was unmarried. Even Annie was shocked – she briefly stopped speaking to her. Sylvia wrote to her and asked her to come to Woodford, where they patched things up. Annie grew very fond of Richard: 'When he began to walk, he used to chase me all over the place. Later he used to write me notes saying, "Please Mrs Barnes, come and have tea with me."'

In later years Sylvia was primarily concerned with fighting fascism, racism and colonialism. She was a vocal supporter of Indian independence, and believed that the hope of the world lay in internationalism, as this extract from her 1926 book *India and Earthly Paradise* shows:

In the days to come peoples, differing as they do, in diet, costume and habits, in work and recreation, under the influence of climate and natural conditions, will serve each other, learn from each other, and enjoy each other's variety free from the hatreds born of the present economic rivalries. When the Northman of the future confronts the people of the far East or South, he will feel neither the mingled fear and contempt of the exploiter of a weaker and more numerous race, nor the jealous hatred of the worker who fears the lower paid competitor will steal his job.

And they who today by reason of class or race are oppressed and exploited, will commingle as friends and comrades with the descendants of those who were once their conquerors and foes. Whilst we must work for Swaraj as a necessary step in the evolution of the peoples of India, and one which leaves them more free than now to unravel their own problems, we must recognise that this is but one step on the road by which they and all peoples must travel. Before us all lies one hope and one goal: mutuality. Whilst competition and exploitation are the basis of the social organism, the expulsion of the foreign exploitation simply means the growth of the native exploitation. Our goal is the end of all exploitation: the world-wide abundance, mutuality and fraternity of the Earthly Paradise.

She devoted the last twenty-five years of her life to protecting Ethiopian independence from Italian rule, launching another newspaper in 1936, the *New Times and Ethiopia News*. In 1956, at the age of 74, the Ethiopian government extended a formal invitation to Sylvia to live in Ethiopia, which she accepted. She was an honoured guest, with two medals and a street named after her in Addis Ababa. When she died in 1960 she was awarded a state funeral in Ethiopia.

Poplar rebels and fallen soldiers

Several former members of the East London Federation of the Suffragettes were involved in the Poplar Rates Rebellion in 1921. Poplar was one of the poorest areas of London and received no government support to tackle the deep poverty found in the borough; instead, any relief efforts were funded by the borough itself under the Poor Law system.

Although the council's costs were much higher than those of wealthy boroughs because of this, Poplar still had to contribute to the London County Council, Metropolitan Police, the Metropolitan Asylum Board and the Metropolitan Water Board at the same rate as richer areas. Faced with a large increase in the rates owed to these bodies, in 1921 the Poplar Council decided not to pay rather than pass the tax burden on to Poplar residents. The London County Council and Metropolitan Asylum Board took the matter to the High Court and in response the council organised a procession of thousands of supporters from Bow, with a banner proclaiming, 'Poplar Borough Council marching to the High Court and possibly to prison'.

Thirty councillors, including Mayor George Lansbury and his daughter-in-law Minnie Lansbury, Julia Scurr and Nellie Cressall, were imprisoned for contempt of court when they refused to pay, although Nellie was released early as she was six months pregnant. The councillors drew huge public support, from local people, neighbouring councils, and trade unions. Minnie Lansbury said: 'I wish the Government joy in its efforts to get this money from the people of Poplar. Poplar will pay its share of London's rates when Westminster, Kensington, and the City do the same.' After six weeks the court bowed to public pressure and the councillors were released on 12 October. They issued a statement that said:

We leave prison as free men and women, pledged only to attend a conference with all parties concerned in the dispute with us about rates ... We feel our imprisonment has been well worth while, and none of us would have done otherwise than we did. We have forced public attention on the question of London rates, and have materially assisted in forcing the Government to call Parliament to deal with unemployment.

Although the Poplar councillors had triumphed (a law was passed shortly afterwards to help equalise tax burdens between boroughs) there was a tragic end to the story. While in prison Minnie Lansbury caught pneumonia and after leaving prison never fully recovered her health. On 1 January 1922 she died, aged just 32. Her death was announced at a thousand-strong meeting at Bow Baths Hall: 'The audience for a moment was stricken silent ... Then out of the silence came a woman's cry of grief, followed by the weeping of many women.' The meeting was abandoned. A few days later a crowd of thousands of mourners, mostly women, stood in the streets as her coffin passed by. George Lansbury wrote a moving tribute to his daughter-in-law in the *Daily Herald*:

Minnie, in her 32 years, crammed double that number of years' work compared with what many of us are able to accomplish. Her glory lies in the fact that with all her gifts and talents one thought dominated her whole being night and day: How shall we help the poor, the weak, the fallen, weary and heavy-laden, to help themselves? When, a soldier like Minnie passes on, it only means their presence is withdrawn, their life and work remaining an inspiration and a call to us each to close the ranks and continue our march breast forward.

She wasn't the only suffrage 'soldier' who passed away in these years. Keir Hardie died in 1915 aged 59, after a series of strokes. Sylvia was devastated. Her memorial in *The Woman's Dreadnought* described him as 'the greatest human being of our time'. And Mrs Savoy, the Bow brushmaker who had been one of the deputation to meet Prime Minister Asquith in 1914, died shortly after the war. Sylvia's accounts reveal a cheerful, determined and deeply generous woman who was loved and respected by her whole community. Although she was very poor and frequently in ill health, she would go to great lengths to help those in need, even adopting two small boys who had been orphaned. 'The streets of Old Ford are colder and greyer with her loss,' Sylvia wrote, sadly. 'One day the women of England will lead us out of the misery and degradation of slumdom and poverty,' wrote George Lansbury. 'And will do so because millions of Mrs Savoys have shown by their lives that it can and will be done.'

Julia Scurr, who had devoted her life to relieving the suffering and poverty endured by the poor people of Poplar, died just six years after the Rates Rebellion in 1927, aged 57. She had been admitted to Bromley Infirmary in the last years of her life as she was deteriorating mentally. Her fellow councillor George Lansbury believed that the treatment she received while in prison was directly responsible for her early death.

After decades of fighting injustice and championing the people of East London, George Lansbury himself passed away in 1940. He had spent the last few years of his life trying to prevent a Second World War, travelling throughout Europe meeting the political leaders of the various countries. In his 1935 book, *Looking Backwards and Forwards*, Lansbury wrote: 'There is one outstanding lesson I have learned, that wealth can only be acquired at the expense of others.'

Political lives

Several of the younger members of the East London Federation of the Suffragettes went on to have careers as Labour politicians. After the Poplar rebellion Nellie Cressall continued her work as a Labour Party activist and eventually followed in George Lansbury's footsteps by becoming Mayor of Poplar in 1943. In 1951, when Nellie was 69 years old (with twenty-six grandchildren and eight great-grandchildren!), she delivered a speech at the annual Labour Party Conference in Scarborough, defending the great strides in living conditions which Labour had brought about since the First World War:

> Years ago after the First World War many, many people in my constituency sat in the dark because they had not got a penny to put in the gas. Today what do I find? People come to me creating about the heavy electricity bills they have to pay! … I have young people coming worrying me for houses … We have got some houses where six families lived once upon a time … Whereas in the old days people would get married, as I did, and be contented in two nice little rooms, today our young people want a home of their own … I get very needled when I hear housewives complaining because they cannot get the best butter. In my day they never knew what it was. And did they get cow's milk? Not on your life! … Did they ever grumble about their meat then? No, because they only had meat once a week and that was Sunday dinner.

Her speech 'roused the audience to prolonged applause and cheering' and drew praise from Aneurin Bevan, who said her speech was the finest at the conference. She died in 1973.

Daisy Parsons also became involved in local politics, and in 1936 became the first woman mayor of West Ham. She was an energetic mayor, attending huge numbers of meetings and engagements. In 1937 she opened Beckton Lido, and drove the first trolley-bus service in West Ham. Less than a month before the trolley-bus adventure, she attended the coronation of George VI at Westminster Abbey, and reported back for the *Stratford Express*:

> I was in a balcony just above the Unknown Warrior's Tomb with other mayors, and although we could not see the actual crowning there was plenty else to see. The great impression to my mind was the splendour of the pageantry and the brilliance of the whole scene, the wonderful tapestries, and the richness of the carpets, the beautiful dresses gorgeous uniforms, and colourful national costumes of the visitors from other countries. The whole made a scene never to be forgotten. I had never witnessed a state procession before, and I don't suppose I shall ever be present at such a ceremony again, and I regard it as an outstanding event in my life.

> I felt too that this was probably the only country in the world where a royal family could move with such perfect freedom among the populace without fear of any untoward happening, and I also felt that the wide representation of all classes and creeds within the Abbey was a wonderful demonstration of the close relationship between the Throne and the people ... The general impression left on her mind was that there was no class distinction in the Abbey where people representative of all sections had met as members of one big united family to witness a great historic event.

The article also notes that the mayor 'had taken the precaution of providing herself with a sandwich, but although she was there from twenty to seven in the morning until five past six at night she never thought about it'.

As well as being a Labour alderman, councillor and mayor, Daisy served as a Justice of the Peace and chaired numerous welfare committees. As chair of the Education Committee she was responsible for the evacuation of children from West Ham during the Second World War, and helped to organise the Women's Voluntary Service in the borough. In 1949 she was awarded the Freedom of the Borough and in 1951 received an MBE for her public service. She died in 1957, after a severe attack of diabetes, aged 67.

Though she didn't receive the same recognition as Nellie Cressall or Daisy Parsons, their fellow suffragette 'Tough' Annie Barnes became a Stepney councillor in 1934 after several years in a similar unofficial role: 'People used to queue outside my door with their problems. It's nice to advise and help people if you can. There were so many awful cases.' In and out of her role as councillor, Annie helped people access state support, challenge bullying officials and confront greedy landlords. She recounts one episode in which a woman came to her in great distress after her landlord had threatened her family with eviction when she asked him to repair the roof, which had fallen in over her son's bedroom. Annie went with her to confront him:

> He lived in North London somewhere. We went there by bus and knocked on the door ... he saw the woman, and shouted, 'YOU!'
>
> I said, very quietly, 'Yes, but it's not her this time. You've dealt with her, now you deal with me. I'm a member of the Public Health Authority and I shall report you. You've had it now. You say you've got no money. You take the rent and you don't do anything, so now you know what to expect.'
>
> He begged of me then. He calmed right down.
>
> 'Oh please, please ...' he said.

I said, 'No, I don't please anybody now,' and we walked out.

At the next meeting of the Public Health Committee I reported it, and asked the Sanitary Inspector to go round and bring a report of what needed to be done to all the houses. My God! They needed everything … We gave him an ultimatum … He had them done up inside and out, even the painting outside, so they showed up the rest of the houses in Grosvenor Street … We frightened the life out of him.

Annie was a councillor in Stepney for fourteen years, as well as setting up a Women's Co-operative Guild and sitting on the board of a number of local charities. Her fascinating memoirs were published in 1980 when she was 92 years old, and she closed by saying:

I'm finished now. I haven't been to a Labour meeting for years because of this arthritis. I've got a few things I could say to our Labour Government! … One thing I would like to do is go to the House of Commons some time. I'd get a seat furthest from the aisle so I'd have plenty of time to say what I wanted before they could drag me out!

Although the East London Federation of the Suffragettes only existed for a few years, it made a tremendous impact, in the East End and beyond. The Federation worked tirelessly to win over the people of East London to the cause of votes for women, and succeeded. They even seem to have won over Prime Minister Herbert Asquith: their meeting with him in June 1914 was a milestone on the road to women's suffrage. But what makes them truly remarkable is the way that they wove themselves into the fabric of East End life, connecting their cause with the everyday lives of the people around them, and then adapting and changing their strategies and priorities to address the concerns of working women. In its short lifetime, the East London Federation of the Suffragettes empowered hundreds of people and inspired thousands more.

It is high time the work of these magnificent women was better known. Although Sylvia Pankhurst was famous in her day – a true radical, a born leader, charismatic, artistic and passionate – she has been overshadowed by her mother Emmeline and sister Christabel Pankhurst. And the other East London Suffragettes are hardly known at all. With this book we aimed to tell their story, and give Adelaide Knight, Minnie Baldock, Julia Scurr, Zelie Emerson, Norah Smyth, Daisy Parsons, Nellie Cressall, Melvina Walker, Charlotte Drake, Minnie Lansbury, Annie Barnes, Rose Pengelly and Mrs Savoy a fraction of the recognition they deserve.

Even so, these names are just the best known of the least known. What the East London Federation of the Suffragettes built in the East End was a true mass movement for women's rights and for equality. They could not have done what they did without the support of many hundreds more women and men, whose names are now lost to us. It seems fitting to end with an excerpt from a poem by working-class writer Ethel Carnie, which was published in *The Woman's Dreadnought* in May 1915. 'Unknown' is about a woman who 'wore just what she would, and had her say':

She set her face against accepted creeds
Because she deemed it right, and them too weak
And old and useless like long-withered reeds.

Her grave is lost beneath the hiding grass;
Her name is graven not on crumbling stone,
But burns immortal 'midst the pioneers,
Although she lived, and fought, and died unknown.

Eleven

WOMEN'S ACTIVISM AFTER THE SUFFRAGETTES

Just as women's activism in East London didn't begin with the suffragettes, it didn't end with them either. Sadly, women's voices are seldom present in the records and recollections of some key moments throughout the twentieth century when the East End took up arms (both literal and metaphorical) against injustice. But women were there.

The Battle of Cable Street

Let's take one of East London's proudest moments, the Battle of Cable Street, as an example. On 4 October 1936, Oswald Moseley's fascist Blackshirts attempted to march from Tower Hill, through Aldgate and Shadwell, a predominantly Jewish neighbourhood at that time. When they arrived at Gardiner's Corner, a crowd of 250,000 gathered to block their path, roaring, 'They Shall Not Pass!' After 6,000 police failed to clear the area, the march was diverted via Cable Street. However, three sets of barricades, including an overturned lorry, had already been set up there. Broken glass and marbles had been strewn across the street, and thousands of local people massed behind each barricade, chanting anti-fascist slogans and fighting back fiercely against the police. Local communist activist Phil Piratin recalled:

> It was along Cable Street that from the roofs and the upper floors, people, ordinary housewives, and elderly women too, were throwing down milk bottles and other weapons and all kinds of refuse that they didn't any longer want in the house onto the police.

Eventually the Police Commissioner instructed Mosley to march his troops west and out of the area, in a humiliating defeat. Thousands of the anti-fascist protestors gathered in Victoria Park to celebrate their victory.

Although the image of housewives throwing rubbish down at the police and the fascists has become an important part of the Cable Street mythology, the occasional reference or photograph clearly shows that women were also in the street, fighting alongside the men. Mick Mindel was a union leader who was there on the day, and in an interview years later he commented that 'women leaders like Sarah Wesker set an example and at the time of the Cable Street battle she was a real inspiration to all of us'.

Sarah Wesker has been all but forgotten now, but in the 1920s she gained a high profile in London as a formidable union organiser, leading famous strikes at the Goodman's, Poliakoff's, Simpson and Rego textile factories. In 1932 she was elected to the Communist Party's Central Committee at the 12th Congress. Fluent in Yiddish and English, she had a reputation as a fiery speaker, 'as if the energy of five men was balled up inside that miniature frame of hers' (Sarah was less than 5 feet tall).

Jack Shaw, another Cable Street battler interviewed in later life, makes a compelling reference to a young woman he saw in the police charge room after they had both been arrested.

> While he was there, he saw a huge policeman drag in a young woman, rip off her blouse and hold his truncheon as if to strike her in the face. She stared straight at him and, with defiance in her voice, said: 'I am not afraid of you'. As the room went quiet, the policeman called her a Jewish bitch and put her in a cell. Jack says she typified the courage and spirit of the women in the anti-fascist struggle.

Finally, Charlie Goodman, just 16 when he was arrested and savagely beaten by the police after climbing a lamp post and shouting to the crowd: 'Don't be yellow bellies, forward, we are winning!', later married a woman who was also there. Joy was only 12 in 1936 but was nonetheless in the front line. They met four years later and she asked if 'he was the nutcase up the lamp post. When he said he was, she knew he was just her type.'

Bengali Housing Action Group

Women were also at the heart of the rent strikes in East London in the 1930s and 1940s, at which the famous Stepney Tenant's Defence League was created. Women are visible everywhere in photos of the protests and barricades, and important work is now being done to illuminate their role – especially Jewish women – in the struggles for decent housing and affordable rents. But in most popular accounts their voices are still missing. The same is largely true of the next wave of struggle for better housing in East London, which was led by the Bengali community of Tower Hamlets, in particular those living in the semi-derelict tenements of Spitalfields.

In the early 1970s the Tower Hamlets' Bengali community grew rapidly as wives and children arrived in Britain to join their husbands and fathers. Facing intense prejudice and racist persecution, the new arrivals formed a community that was close knit, culturally and geographically. More, and better, housing was urgently needed. Reports from the time describe whole families crammed into one or two rooms, with broken plumbing and rats who nipped the feet of sleeping children.

However, Bengali families experienced discrimination when they applied for council housing, an experience confirmed by an independent 1984 report commissioned by the Greater London Council which revealed deeply entrenched racism in the system. Their housing options were also limited by the racist attacks to which non-white families became vulnerable when they were allocated a house on an estate entirely populated by white people. In frustration and desperation, many families joined the squatters' movement, and began to occupy empty buildings. Housing activist Terry Fitzpatrick and members of the Race Today Collective, Farrukh Dhondy and Mala Sen, worked with the Spitalfields community to identify and break into empty properties. In February 1976 they brought together seventy families who formed the Bengali Housing Action Group (BHAG). A few weeks later they broke into the Pelham Buildings, which were awaiting GLC redevelopment. In three months forty-one families were living there. Through the activities of the BHAG and other housing campaigners, the dire situation of many immigrant families was highlighted and improvements were made to tackle the racism inherent in the council housing system.

Many Bengali women were not allowed to take part in activities outside the home, but played an important role even so. Housing campaigner Charlie Forman commented: 'It has been women who have been most militant about staying in the Spitalfields area. They stand to lose more than their men, and have frequently dissuaded the men from signing for distant flats even when there is apparently no other choice.'

The most visible woman involved in BHAG was the remarkable Mala Sen, who eloped from India to England with Farrukh Dhondy in 1965 when she was 17. In London, Mala took up sewing jobs in sweatshops to earn a living, and the couple became active in a number of equality campaigns, especially around race relations, housing and immigration. Later Sen became a television documentary maker and writer, and published a successful biography of Phoolan Devi, the 'Bandit Queen'. Sen shared Sylvia Pankhurst's belief that supporting people to claim their rights and empower themselves was the best way to achieve political change. She said: 'When you are a political activist, you empower other people to take their chance to empower themselves. Once they have empowered themselves, you say, "Okay sweetie, now it's your household, you look after it, I'm going."'

A fair wage

A few years earlier, further east in Dagenham, another group of women had picked up the Federation's call for equal pay. Sewing machinists at the Ford Motor Car Company worked in poor conditions for low pay, making car seat covers. Although the work required skill and concentration (the sewing machines had no guards, and injuries were common) Ford announced it was regrading the machinists' pay as grade B (less skilled production jobs), instead of grade C (more skilled production jobs), and that they would be paid 15 per cent less than the B rate received by men. The women complained, but the company wouldn't budge. Bernie Passington, of the Transport & General Worker's Union, who fought with the machinists, said, 'Like any group of workers, if they're going to take no notice, better do something what makes them take notice.'

The women voted to strike, and walked out on 7 June 1968, bringing production at the entire company to a standstill. Soon the Dagenham machinists were joined by the Ford Halewood Plant in Liverpool. One of the strikers, Sheila Douglas, remembers how it felt: 'We didn't think we were that strong … It was a surprise to us as well as everybody else. We didn't think we were going to fetch the whole Ford Empire to its knees, as you might say, but that's what happened eventually. And it was all down to us, us ladies.'

While many of the trade unions, members of the general public and even some of the women's husbands opposed the strike, they also found support from other working women, and the dispute drew the attention of Barbara Castle, then Secretary of State for Trade and Industry. Castle convened a meeting between ministers, the union and the company, where Ford agreed to raise the women's wages to 100 per cent of grade B rate over two years. The union settled for this, but the machinists were unsatisfied, as their work was still deemed to be 'less skilled'. It wasn't to be regraded until after a second strike in 1984.

However, the strike had highlighted the gap between women's and men's pay, and persuaded Barbara Castle to introduce legislation to end this injustice. The Equal Pay Act was introduced in 1970. Although the gender pay gap persists today, the Equal Pay Act has been an important tool for employees to challenge direct pay discrimination.

Another important strike took place in 1972 at the Ministry of Defence, led by East Ender and union activist May Hobbs. May set up the campaigning group Cleaners Action to support cleaners to organise and secure better pay and conditions. In July 1972 ten cleaners came out on strike at the Ministry of Defence office in Fulham, calling for a £3 increase on the £12.50 they were paid for a 45-hour week, as well as union recognition. Cleaners Action and members of the women's liberation movement set up a 24-hour picket and worked to gather messages of support. Early in August, twenty more women from a building in Whitehall joined, with the same demands, and another twenty the week after that. Shortly afterwards the civil service caved in, and the new pay was fixed at £16.50 a week plus a 50p night allowance for a normal week's work.

In her autobiography *Born To Struggle,* May comments:

> The great thing was we had won in this case and shown what might be done. We had got the whole subject aired in the press and in the House of Commons by such M.P.s as Lena Jager and Joe Ashton and people knew a bit more about what went on in their offices, while they were snugly tucked in their beds, to keep things nice and civilized for them when they got in for work.

Cleaners Action were supported by the emerging Women's Liberation movement, through which women were coming together to fight for feminist causes in East London as they were all over the country. In Newham, Anna Davin, Nell Myers and Beatrix Campbell founded the Stratford Women's Liberation Group in the early 1970s. The Women's Liberation workshop created a newsletter called *Shrew*, each issue of which was edited by a different local group. This allowed the editors to go into more depth about local issues (for example the availability of contraception) than national feminist publications like *Spare Rib*. Shrew was a mixture of news, features, poems, notices and political cartoons, reminiscent of *The Woman's Dreadnought*.

Women against racism

But it was not only class-based and sexist oppression which East End women were struggling against during the 1970s: women played a part in the anti-racist movement too. In 1974 the National Front gained 5,000 votes in Newham. The National Front targeted East and South East London, selling racist newspapers on Brick Lane, and installing their central office on Great Eastern Street. Eastside Community Heritage have interviewed many women involved in anti-racist activism at this time, and Jenny Bourne recalled how thousands of East Londoners took to the streets on 13 August 1977 to bar the National Front from marching through South East London. That day Bourne stewarded for Women Against Racism and Fascism at what became known as the Battle of Lewisham:

> We mobilised magnificently for Lewisham. I mean loads of women. Far more than was in Women against Racism and Fascism. Lewisham really got a hell of a lot of women out. The NF had sort of organised on this side street, and they were trying to walk down into the centre of Lewisham. And because we were an organised group, and because there was quite a lot of us, I can't remember how many hundred, we were asked to block their way, so we all sat down. And the police on horseback had decided that they had to give the NF the right to march, and because we didn't move we all got quite badly beaten. 'Cos they just sort of beat a line through, through the group. The police were just incredibly violent. I was just standing there

and they picked me up on a riot shield and threw me across the road, and I landed on my back.

In the late 1970s and early 1980s, several organisations were established in East London to empower women, particularly women of colour. These included the East London Black Women's Organisation (founded in 1979 by Ama Gueye), the Newham Asian Women's Project and the Jagonari centre in Whitechapel, both established in 1987. Many of these organisations provided advice and support around domestic abuse and other forms of violence against women, from legal representation to counselling to space in a refuge. The Jagonari Centre was founded by a group of Bangladeshi women, and aimed to challenge common representations of Bangladeshi women as submissive. It takes its name from a famous Bengali poem, 'Rise Up Women' by Nazrul Islam, which urges women to rise up against injustice.

Like the East London Federation of the Suffragettes' Women's Hall at 400 Old Ford Road, the centre also provides opportunities for education and skills training, kitchens, affordable childcare and play facilities, as well as social events. One of the founders, Shila Thakur, spoke about their aims in a 2006 interview for the Swadinhata Trust:

> What we wanted to set up was something that involved child care with training. You can't have training without child care. And that was something that we knew back in the early 80s … So we set up a central place where there could be lots of different kinds of training, and place as a meeting place, somewhere you could go … We wanted to have this big open place where women could go, and café-like kitchens.

Recent years

Housing was back on the agenda in East London in the 1990s, and women played a major part in the revived squatting movement, which battled with Hackney Council in 1993, as well as anarchist and environmental campaigns. The 2000s and 2010s have seen a resurgence of feminist activism, with the appearance of local groups such as East London Feminists, East London Fawcett, Abortion Rights East London, as well as a crop of hip new Women's Institute branches, including the Shoreditch Sisters, Dalston Darlings and Stow Roses, who campaign against violence and media sexism. Grassroots groups like the Stratford-based Focus E15 Mothers continue to campaign for better housing and support for working mothers.

In 2013, three significant events took place on the theme of women's history: on International Women's Day, the Women's Library in Aldgate was occupied in protest of the library's imminent removal to the London School of Economics in Holborn. Activists from various feminist groups, as well as UK Uncut, Occupy and Disabled People Against the Cuts formed a coalition to try and keep the Women's Library in East London, and managed to occupy it for two days before they were forcibly removed by the police. One of the women who took part in the occupation, university lecturer Josie Foreman, commented:

> Holding onto the history of women's struggle for equality becomes even more important in a moment like this, when the government is closing women's refuges and shutting down children's centres. The Women's Library reminds us that these are hard-won gains for which women have fought for centuries. We will not allow them to be taken away from us so easily. Acting in the tradition of the suffragettes, we are willing to

take direct action for what we believe in. In this time of savage austerity, we do indeed need 'Deeds, not Words'.

On Saturday, 8 June 2013, the East London Feminists held a march in suffragette costume through the East End, followed by a rally in Victoria Park. Although the crowd was small, the date was significant, as it marked the centenary of the death of Emily Wilding Davison, who walked into the path of the King's horse at the Epsom Derby in 1913.

And finally, on Saturday, 6 July 2013, historian Louise Raw organised a day-long festival of speeches, music, comedy and debate at the Bishopsgate Institute near Liverpool Street, to celebrate the 125th anniversary of the Matchwomen's Strike at the Bryant and May factory in Bow. Hundreds of people attended on the day, and many more heard the story of the 1888 strike for the first time through the press coverage the event generated.

Which brings us full circle. From the courageous matchwomen of 1888 to the women in 2013 who are inspired by them, the story of women's activism in East London is rich and varied. The East End has a long, proud history of protest and action, of communities coming together – despite their differences and their poverty – to defy injustice and fight for a brighter future. Women are as much a part of that history as men, and sometimes they have led the way.

ACKNOWLEDGEMENTS

Norah Smyth's photographs reproduced with kind permission of Paul Isolani Smyth from the Estelle Sylvia Pankhurst collection at the International Institute of Social History (Amsterdam).

Grateful thanks to Helen Pankhurst, Paul Isolani Smyth, and Tower Hamlets Local History Library and Archives.

While every effort has been made to trace the owners of copyright material, the author would like to apologise for any omissions and will be pleased to incorporate missing acknowledgements in any future editions.

BIBLIOGRAPHY

Adie, Kate. *Fighting on the Home Front: The Legacy of Women in WWI*.
London: Hodder & Stoughton, 2013

Archer, Thomas. *The Pauper, The Thief and the Convict*. London:
Groombridge, 1865

Barnes, Annie. *Tough Annie*. London: Stepney Books, 1980

Connelly, Katherine. *Sylvia Pankhurst: Suffragette, Socialist and
Scourge of Empire*. London: Pluto Press, 2013

Crawford, Elizabeth. *The Women's Suffrage Movement: A Reference
Guide 1866-1928*. London: UCL Press, 1998

Davis, Mary. *Sylvia Pankhurst: A Life In Radical Politics*. London: Pluto
Press, 1999

Franklin, Miles. Eds Jill Roe and Margaret Bettison. *A Gregarious
Culture: Topical Writings of Miles Franklin*. Australia: Univ. of
Queensland Press, 2001

Kenney, Annie. *Memories of a Militant*. London: E. Arnold & Co., 1924

Kenney, Annie and Frederick Pethick-Lawrence. *Character Sketch and
Prison Faces*. London: Labour Record and Review, 1907

London, Jack. *The People of the Abyss*. London: Macmillan, 1903

Montefiore, Dora B. *From a Victorian to a Modern*. London: E. Archer, 1927

Pankhurst, Sylvia. *The Home Front*. London: The Cressett Library, 1987

Pankhurst, Sylvia. *The Suffragette Movement*. London: Virago, 1988
——— *India and the Earthly Paradise*. Bombay: 'Bombay Chronicle' Press, Sunshine Publishing House, 1926

Randolph Churchill, Jennie. *Women's War Work*. London: C Arthur Pearson, 1916

Raw, Louise. *Striking a Light: The Bryant and May Matchwomen and their Place in History*. London: Bloomsbury, 2009

Rocker, Rudolf. *The London Years*. London: AK Press, 2005

Rosen, Andrew. R*ise Up, Women!: The Militant Campaign of the Women's Social and Political Union*. London: Routledge, 1974

Sandhu, Sukhdev. *London Calling: How Black and Asian Writers Imagined a City*. London: Harper Collins, 2003

Silvester, Victor. *Dancing Is My Life: The Autobiography of Victor Silvester*. London: Heinemann, 1958

Taylor, Rosemary. *In Letters of Gold*. London: Stepney Books, 1993

Winslow, Barbara. *Sylvia Pankhurst: Sexual Politics And Political Activism*, London: Routledge, 1996

Wollstonecraft, Mary, *A Vindication of the Rights of Woman*. London: J. Johnson, 1792

INDEX

Also from The History Press

CELEBRATING WOMEN'S HISTORY

Lightning Source UK Ltd.
Milton Keynes UK
UKOW04f1116210814

237299UK00006B/73/P